I0806905

USBORNE

UNDERSTANDING PHYSICS

Written by
Rachel Firth,
Minna Lacey and
Darran Stobbart

Illustrated by
El Primo Ramón

Physics expert:
Daisy Shearer

Designed by
Jamie Ball

Contents

Usborne Quicklinks

For links to websites where you can find out more about physics, and explore some of the ideas in this book with videos, experiments and activities, go to **usborne.com/Quicklinks** and type in the title of this book.

Please follow the internet safety guidelines at Usborne Quicklinks. Children should be supervised online.

What is physics?

Physics is a branch of science which is all about how the universe works – and absolutely everything in it. This turns out to cover rather a *lot* of things – from the stars in the night sky to riding a bicycle.

Physicists like to simplify things to make them easier to understand. So they describe the whole universe using just three terms – matter, energy and forces.

1. Matter

Matter is the name physicists use for *stuff* – the things you can see and touch. *Everything* around you is made from matter...

One thing physicists have discovered about matter is that it's all made of tiny, *tiny* pieces, called **atoms**. Atoms are so small that you can only see them using incredibly powerful microscopes. It's how atoms are *arranged* that makes matter behave the way it does.

Take this glass of water...

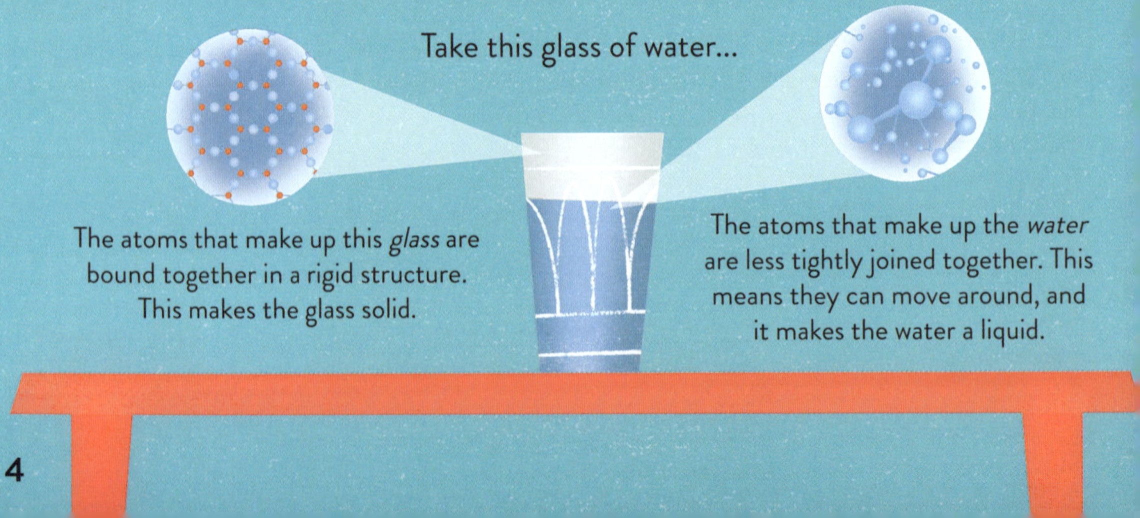

The atoms that make up this *glass* are bound together in a rigid structure. This makes the glass solid.

The atoms that make up the *water* are less tightly joined together. This means they can move around, and it makes the water a liquid.

2. Energy

Matter doesn't do very much by itself – you need **energy** to make things happen. Energy is the word used to describe the ability of matter *to do work.* In physics, doing work means *changing* or *moving.* For example...

A skateboard won't move on its own.

When skaters kick on the ground, they give the skateboard movement energy – known as kinetic energy – allowing it to *move.*

The water in this pan doesn't do anything by itself.

Heating the water adds heat energy to it. This makes the water boil and some of it *changes* into steam.

Wood contains chemical energy, but a log can't do anything with it by itself.

When the log burns, its chemical energy is changed into heat and light energy – and some of the wood *changes* into ash.

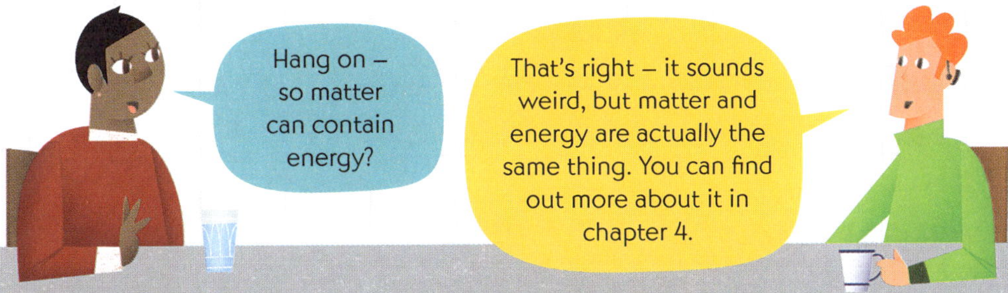
Hang on – so matter can contain energy?
That's right – it sounds weird, but matter and energy are actually the same thing. You can find out more about it in chapter 4.

3. Forces

Physicists use the word **force** to talk about how matter interacts with *other matter.* Forces are always a *push* or a *pull.*

Gravity is a force that *pulls* things to the ground – and makes them fall.

Magnetism is another force. Magnets *pushing* against each other can make a train float.

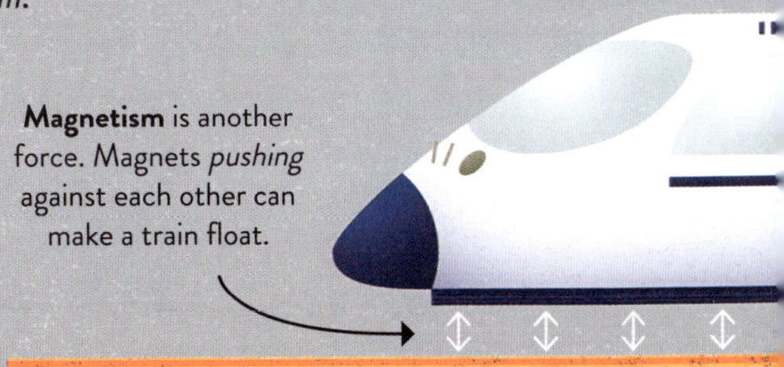

Asking questions

Throughout human history, people have been curious about the world. To satisfy that curiosity, they developed scientific ways of thinking. The first step was to ask questions, such as “What’s that yellow ball in the sky?”

For thousands of years, people tracked the movements of the Sun, Moon and stars. It helped them to determine the best time to plant and harvest crops.

Why does the Sun *always* rise from that spot at this time of year – *every* year?
That must be how the Sun God likes to do things.
It will start getting cold soon – can you two *please* stop pondering the gods and help with the harvest?

They explained the movements of these heavenly objects by telling stories of gods.

Around 2,500 years ago the ancient Greeks started to try to understand how the world worked – *without* the idea of gods. They believed that humans could understand anything.

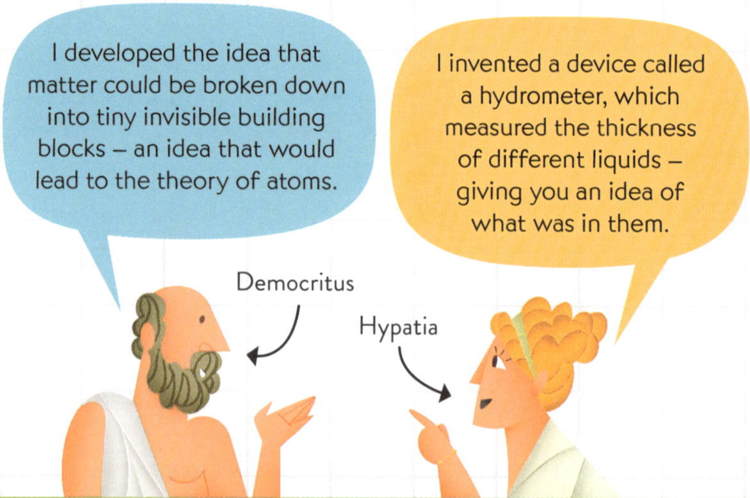

I developed the idea that matter could be broken down into tiny invisible building blocks – an idea that would lead to the theory of atoms.
I invented a device called a hydrometer, which measured the thickness of different liquids – giving you an idea of what was in them.
Democritus
Hypatia

The ancient Greeks spent a lot of time thinking – and arguing – about different ideas.

Ancient Greeks weren't the only ones asking these questions. Ideas were being developed across ancient China and India, too.

I investigated the properties of magnetic metals, and invented the first compass.
Shen Kuo
I was the first to suggest that the Earth rotated to give us day and night.
Aryabhata

From the 8th to the 14th century, across the Middle East, northern Africa and southern Spain, there was a terrific quest for scientific knowledge.

This led to a leap in scientific understanding, and is known as the Islamic Golden Age.

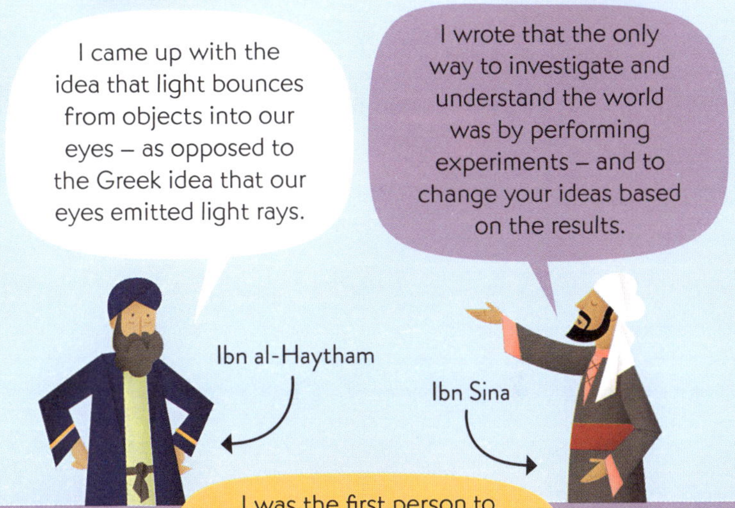
I came up with the idea that light bounces from objects into our eyes – as opposed to the Greek idea that our eyes emitted light rays.
Ibn al-Haytham
I wrote that the only way to investigate and understand the world was by performing experiments – and to change your ideas based on the results.
Ibn Sina

From the 16th to the 19th century, there was a Scientific Revolution in Europe. Discoveries about the nature of the world were being made constantly.

I developed the theory of gravity to explain why things fell towards the Earth.
Isaac Newton
I was the first person to show the link between electricity and magnetism.
Hans Christian Ørsted
I worked on understanding what made some objects radioactive, and not others. Read more in chapter 4.
Marie Curie

By the end of the Scientific Revolution, many thought the job of physics was finished – that everything had been discovered. But people kept trying to understand the world. It turned out there was still a *lot* to uncover.

Physics is everywhere

Physics today covers a huge range of subjects. To make things easier, physicists break the subjects down into different **branches**, which overlap a lot.

Classical mechanics

How objects move when forces act on them.

A rocket taking off

Kicking a ball

Comets hurtling through space

Thermodynamics

The study of heat and energy and how they can be used.

Refrigerator removing heat

Sunlight heating the air making the wind blow

Car engines burning fuel to move

Electromagnetism

The study of electricity and magnetism, and the relationship between them.

Super-fast trains floating on magnets

Using spinning magnets to generate electricity

The magnetic field around the Earth

Optics

The study of the properties of light and what light can be used for.

Telescopes studying distant stars and planets

Arranging light to create 3D holograms

Sending messages using beams of light inside cables

Acoustics

The study of how sound is made, how it travels, and what it can be used for.

Ultrasound is outside of human hearing and can be used to look inside people's bodies.

Using sound to peer into the depths of the ocean

Relativity

The study of the relationship between space and time.

Relativity can be hard to wrap your head around!

Space and time are part of the same thing – spacetime.

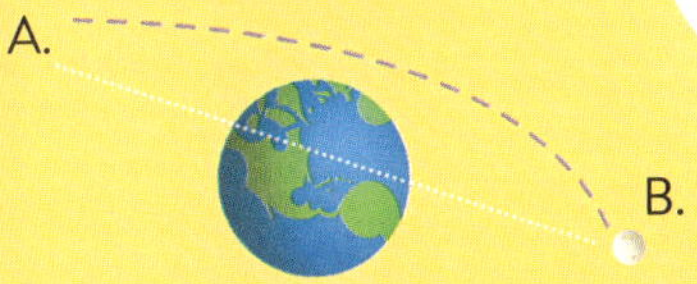

Time moves differently, depending on how fast YOU are moving.

Do black holes bend time as well as space?

Particle physics

The study of radioactivity and the particles that make up atoms.

Nuclear power generated by splitting atoms

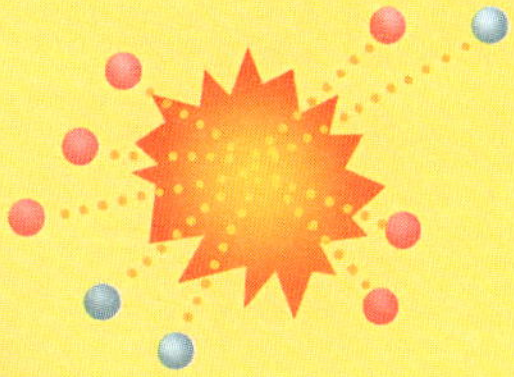

Using radioactive atoms to tell how old something is

Seeing inside people using X-rays

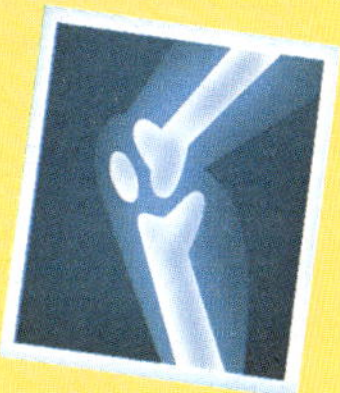

Quantum mechanics

Quantum mechanics is about the *weirdest* science ever gets...

The study of the smallest forms of matter and energy.

When you make a decision, there might be another "you" that makes the *opposite* one.

Teleporting information instantly across massive distances

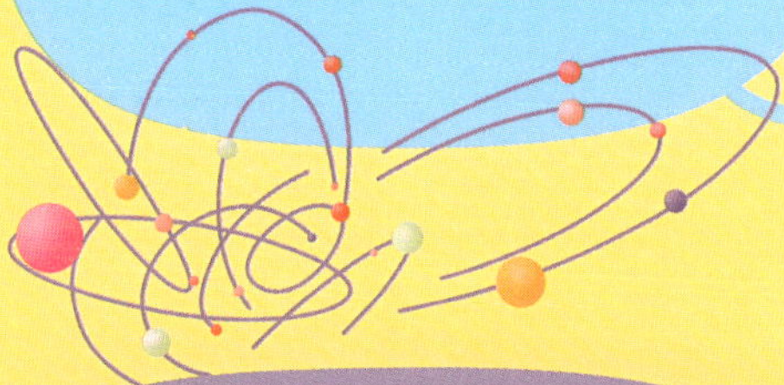

Harnessing the strange properties of particles to help build faster computers

Cosmology

The study of space and the history of the universe.

The Milky Way galaxy has a black hole in the middle of it.

The universe is getting bigger – and it started out very, very small.

Hunting for other planets with the right conditions for life to survive

Don't worry: throughout this book, we'll explain what words such as "quantum" mean.

What do physicists do?

Physicists ask questions – and then set about trying to find answers. Some physics is done using experiments, and some is done with a pencil and paper, but ALL physics needs *curiosity*.

A physicist's journey begins with a question.
Hmm, I wonder what makes rainbows happen?

Then they think about possible answers. When scientists have an idea about how something might work, it's called a **hypothesis**.
Think about it! There are no bad ideas.
Perhaps it's the angle of the sunlight that's causing rainbows?
Maybe raindrops are letting off different shades of light...
I think there are lots of different types of fireflies up there!
Maybe it's leprechauns.
I think there are *some* bad ideas.
?

Rainbows happen when it's been raining. Maybe light gets split up by the water somehow?
?
Now *that* sounds like a hypothesis.

A hypothesis needs proof before you can trust it, so physicists design and run **experiments** to test their ideas. Without proof, it's just a very clever sounding idea.

Well it looks like a convincing idea to me.
But how can we be sure?
...I've got an idea of how to test it.
To the laboratory!

During an experiment, scientists try to make sure they can control everything that might affect their results. These things are known as **variables**.

If we shine light into this spray of water, we should be able to see if it makes a rainbow.
How will we know it's *our* light that's being split up and not sunlight from the windows?
We can control *that* variable by closing all the curtains.
And how do we control the leprechaun variable?
Go away, please.

Scientists record everything they see during the experiment, and then do it again. And again. And ***again***.
Look! When we shine the light through the water, it splits into a rainbow.
Ooooo!
So it seems... but to be **sure** that is what's happening, we should try it a few more times.
Let's get some other scientists to see if they get the same results, too.

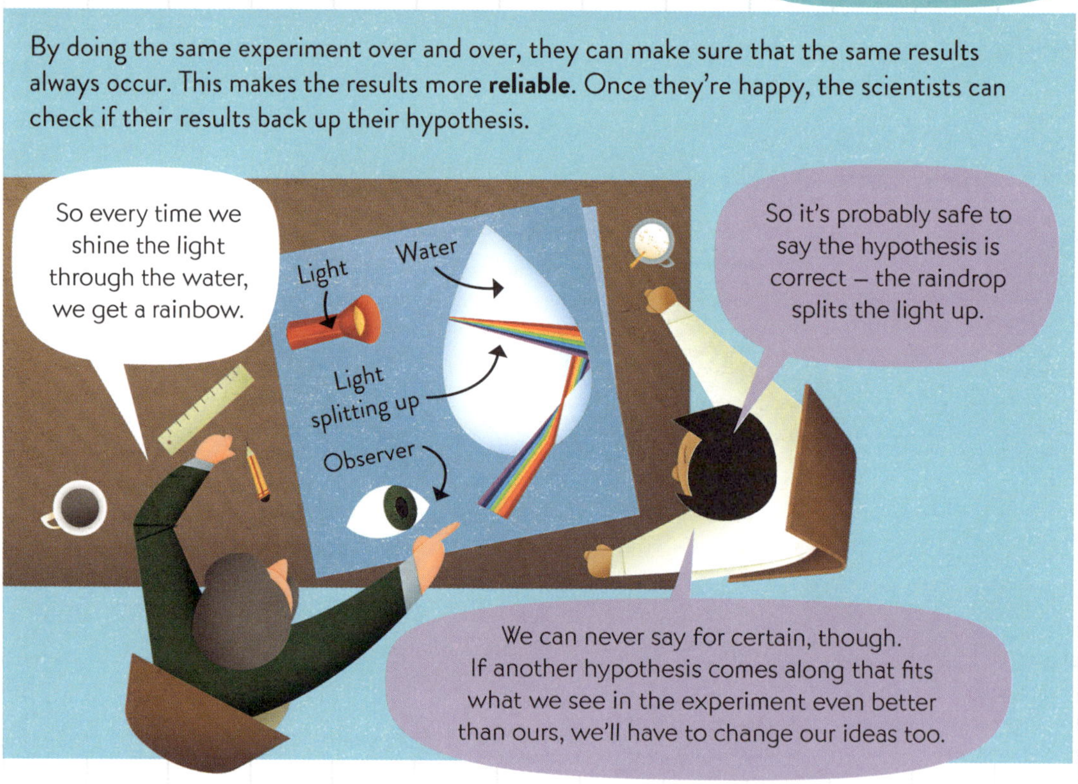
By doing the same experiment over and over, they can make sure that the same results always occur. This makes the results more **reliable**. Once they're happy, the scientists can check if their results back up their hypothesis.
So every time we shine the light through the water, we get a rainbow.
Light
Water
Light splitting up
Observer
So it's probably safe to say the hypothesis is correct – the raindrop splits the light up.
We can never say for certain, though. If another hypothesis comes along that fits what we see in the experiment even better than ours, we'll have to change our ideas too.

If the experiment shows the hypothesis works, it becomes known as a **scientific theory**. If a hypothesis doesn't match the results, it has to be thrown out. This process is called the **experimental method**.
It's one of the core ideas of physics.

Equations, mathematics and physics

Physicists spend their time hunting for simple facts about the universe, and they've found that it can often be described using numbers and mathematics.
An **equation** is a *mathematical fact* that shows the link between things.

$$s = \frac{d}{t}$$

This equation is for calculating speed. It says that speed (s) is always equal to (=) the distance moved (d) divided by the time taken to move that distance (t).

Measuring the speed of something can be tricky. But measuring distance and time are easier. An equation tells you what math to use with those two numbers to give you the speed.

During experiments, scientists measure things – such as time or distance – precisely, using numbers. Equations use letters and symbols to represent those values before they've been measured. Some equations are simple, but as the physics gets more complicated, so do the equations used to talk about it.

$$\frac{-\hbar^2}{2m}\frac{\partial^2\Psi}{\partial x^2} = i\hbar\frac{\partial\Psi}{\partial t}$$

This is an equation used in quantum mechanics – one of the strangest and most complex branches of physics.

It uses letters and symbols to describe the properties of things so small that they're impossible to see.

The world of quantum mechanics involves all the tiniest things we've ever discovered – things that are much tinier than human beings can ever see. At these sizes, matter and energy behave in ways that can be unexpected.

No one knows exactly why the universe follows mathematical rules – but it does.

We can use math to describe things we find it impossible to imagine. You'll see!

Why are the Earth, Moon and planets shaped like spheres?

Why is it so hard to steer a fully loaded shopping cart?

What's so useful about friction?

If the Earth is spinning, how come it feels as if we're stationary?

Chapter 1
FORCES & MOTION

One of the great mysteries of the world is something people rarely stop to think about. It's this: what makes everything move? To physicists the answer is simple – *forces*. If something speeds up or changes direction, it's because of a force – from a bat hitting a ball to a breeze turning the blades of a wind turbine.

Understanding forces and learning rules about them helps us create many incredible machines and buildings. This is all part of a branch of physics called **mechanics**. But sometimes forces make things behave unpredictably, undermining any of the rules that try to explain them...

Are you moving *right now?*

As you read these words, you may think you're stationary. But in fact the Earth is moving through space at a startling 1,040mph as it travels around the Sun. It's also spinning at a dizzying 730mph. It doesn't *feel* as if you're moving, *but you are.*

It's a little like when you're sitting in a moving train.

Feels still (mostly)...
Boing!
...but actually moving.

When a train moves at a steady speed, people don't feel as if they are moving. But they ARE moving – relative to the ground outside. Physicists like to ask "*relative to what* are things moving?" Watch out for this idea again on page 44.

Stopping and starting

Dad, watch out!
A deer!
SQUEAL
SCREECH

If you apply a force to an object, the object changes speed or direction. Sounds simple, right? But daily experience shows that when people and objects are moving, they'd rather continue moving in the same direction. And if they're still, they'd rather stay still. This resistance to change is what physicists call **inertia**.

Understanding inertia has lots of practical uses. For instance, airbags in cars work by countering the effect of inertia. This invention has saved thousands of lives.

When a car stops suddenly, the driver carries on moving forwards due to inertia.

The crash triggers an airbag to inflate and this spreads out the force of the impact. It also stops the driver from hitting the front window.

Airbag
SMASH!
SMASH!

Pushing things around

If you've ever pushed a cart around a supermarket, you'll know that the more things you put in your cart, the bigger the force needed to move it.

Hmphhh!

Similarly, if you push an empty cart with the *same* force you use to push a full one, the empty one speeds up very quickly. It has a higher **acceleration**.

However, once a heavy cart gets going, it's harder to make it stop. That's because it has more *oomph* thrusting it forward. This is known as its **momentum**.

Opposite forces

If you lift up this book, you'll feel its weight pushing back on your hand.

Similarly, if you press your hand on a table, you can feel the same thing. It's the force of the table pressing back against you. It's of *equal* power, and is directly *opposite*.

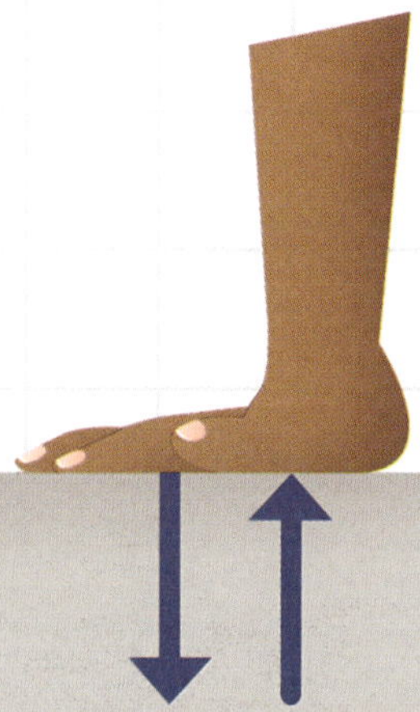

The harder you press, the greater the force in response.

Forces exerting an equal and opposite force is the reason why many things move. It's how things like walking work, it's how wheels work, and it's also how rowing a boat works.

As I row, I push water *backward* with the oars.
And that's what makes the boat move *forward* in the opposite direction.

When a car is moving, the tires on the wheels push *backward* against the road. This produces an equal and opposite force *forward* – called **thrust**.

Newton and newtons

About 400 years ago, English physicist Isaac Newton attempted to pin down *precise* rules about how things move, which he called "the laws of motion." His work was so influential, physicists today measure the strength of a force in units called **newtons**. Thanks to Newton's laws, engineers have been able to design and build amazing things.

Bridges have to stand up to forces from all sorts of directions. These can all be calculated using Newton's laws.
Skyscrapers are designed to sway in the wind, and have deep foundations so they don't fall down.

In fact, Newton's laws don't hold in *all* situations – but they work well enough that engineers can design buildings and bridges that don't fall down. Perhaps being 100% right isn't the most important thing in physics...

But I want to explain how *everything* moves, not just on Earth, but EVERYWHERE in the universe!

Newton's aim was to explain forces on Earth *and* in space. The key force that helped him to understand how the Earth, the Sun and all the planets move is known as **gravity**. But this was where Newton's laws seemed to break down, and he never quite got to the bottom of it. In fact, physicists today still struggle to understand how gravity works. Turn the page to see what we DO know.

The force of gravity

Gravity is a force that pulls things towards each other. It exists between *all* objects: between any object and the Earth, between the planets and the Sun, and between every rock and star in the universe.

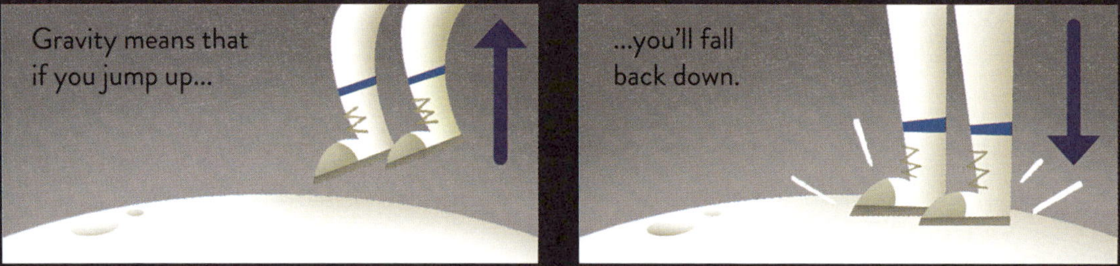
Gravity means that if you jump up...
...you'll fall back down.

For a force that affects us so strongly, you might be surprised to learn that gravity is weak around most things. It's almost impossible to measure gravity between small objects, such as a pen and a book, because it's such a tiny force. But it becomes significant around **MASSIVE** objects, such as the Earth. That's because the *bigger* the amount of matter in an object, the *stronger* its gravitational pull.

Predicting the future

Newton's laws and his study of gravity allowed him to calculate the path of planets and comets as they passed through space. This included how often a particular comet – Halley's comet – would be close enough to Earth to be visible.

The Royal Observatory, Greenwich, 1680
According to my calculations, your comet will not be visible again until 1755!
What a terrible shame – we'll be dead by then.
Newton
Halley

But there were things Newton couldn't predict, such as the orbit of the planet Mercury. The pull of gravity from the Sun and other planets is so strong, that it shifts Mercury's orbit as it passes close by each of them. This wasn't understood until Einstein came up with a *new* theory of gravity, 300 years later (see page 50).

Orbits

Gravity is what lets things orbit the Earth, such as the International Space Station (ISS). But despite the Earth pulling on it, the ISS *doesn't* plunge down to Earth. That's because it's moving so fast – at 17,000mph – it has enough momentum moving it forward and keeping it up.

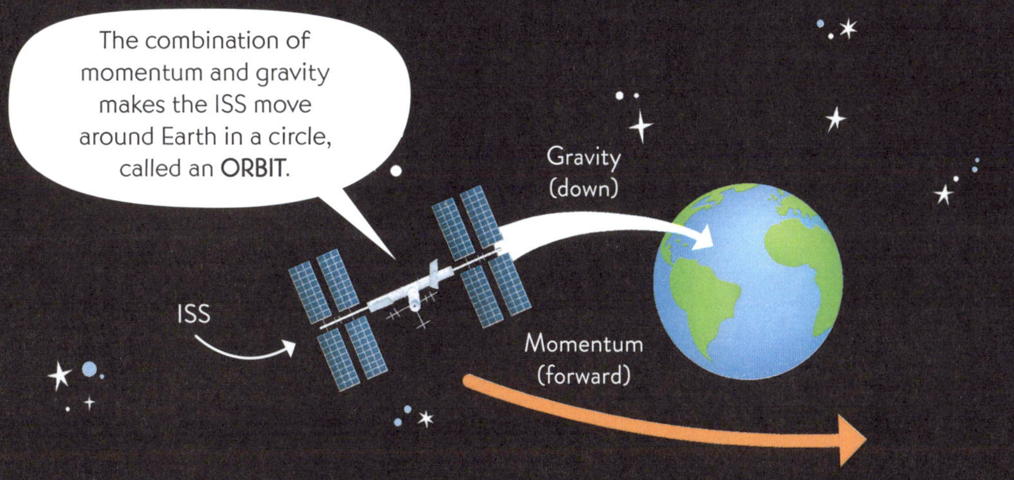
The combination of momentum and gravity makes the ISS move around Earth in a circle, called an ORBIT.
Gravity (down)
ISS
Momentum (forward)

Why are planets round?

Why are all planets round, and not, say, banana-shaped? This is because of gravity, too. Gravity pulls all the matter that makes up each planet in towards its center.

Planets began life as small bits of rock, ice and gas that bumped into each other...

...and clumped together, over BILLIONS of years.
Gradually, these clumps pulled more matter towards the middle...

...until they started to form spheres.

Movement and energy

OK, so things move because forces make them move. But what actually IS movement? An odd question, but one that physicists answer with the word **energy**. All forms of movement are an example of one *type* of energy, called **kinetic energy**.

CRASH
BOSH
SPIN

Imagine kicking a ball. The force of your kick sets the ball in motion, but for the whole time the ball is moving, it's relying on kinetic energy. And where did that energy come from? Well, that's the start of a long chain of questions that leads all the way back to the origin of the universe.

The energy in the ball...
...came from the energy used to make your leg kick.
That energy came from the food you ate.
And that food came from some plants...
...that were able to grow by absorbing energy from sunlight.
The Sun's energy comes from its atoms constantly smashing into each other.
And those atoms, originally, came into being when all the matter that makes up the universe popped into existence.

Energy is something that *can never be created or destroyed*. But it CAN change from one type to another, and be transfered from one set of matter to another. Understanding this has helped people design all sorts of machines and tools that *move* energy around.

Rubbing two sticks together to create a spark changes **chemical energy** in the wood...
...into **heat** and **light energy** in a flame.

Farming uses the fact that plants turn sunlight into chemical energy...
MUNCH
...to make food.

Chemical energy from fuel can be changed into kinetic energy – and heat and **sound energy**... by the engine of this rocket-powered car.

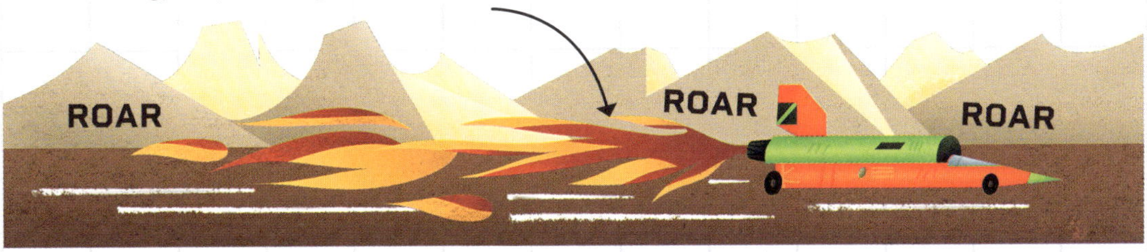

ROAR
ROAR
ROAR

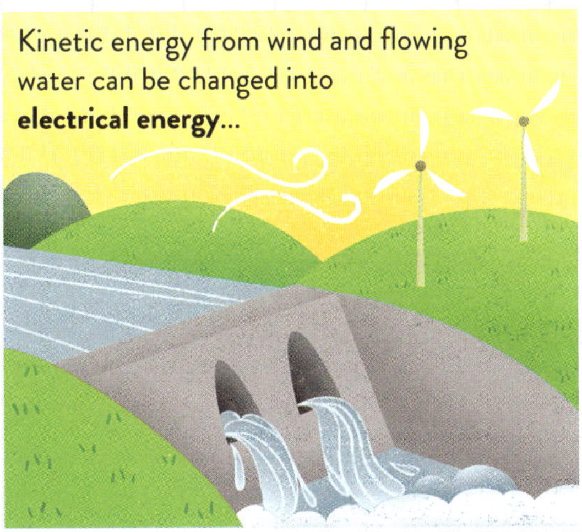

Kinetic energy from wind and flowing water can be changed into **electrical energy**...

...which can be changed into light and sound and heat energy.
VROOM
SCREECH
My controller feels wicked hot!

But no one really knows what energy IS, or if it even makes sense to think of energy as a "thing." You can read more about this in Chapter 4.

Chaos and order

Let's look at the big picture. Energy makes atoms move around inside matter – creating heat which is released and absorbed – or lost – into the surroundings. This process makes ordered matter, that is made of neatly arranged atoms, become more chaotic. How chaotic, or *disordered*, things are depends on what physicists call **entropy**.

A living thing, such as a tree, is highly complex and ordered.

100 years later, it might have fallen down and broken into pieces, rotting in the ground.

Compare the atoms and energy inside the original tree, with the atoms in the broken parts and the energy released into the surroundings. The total amount of energy has stayed the same, but the tree is now in pieces, and those pieces can NEVER be put back.

This pattern happens everywhere: a rock gradually cracks and crumbles, food goes bad and decays. This is the result of a law of something physicists call **thermodynamics**. The law says that as time goes by, things get more disordered and more chaotic. *And there's no going back.*

Oh no! If only I could put my eggs back together.

Force and matter

As far as we know, energy and forces only affect physical objects – things made of *matter*. This has interesting consequences for how objects interact with each other. For example, for something to float, it's less important how *big* it is, but more important *how tightly packed* its matter is – or how **dense** it is.

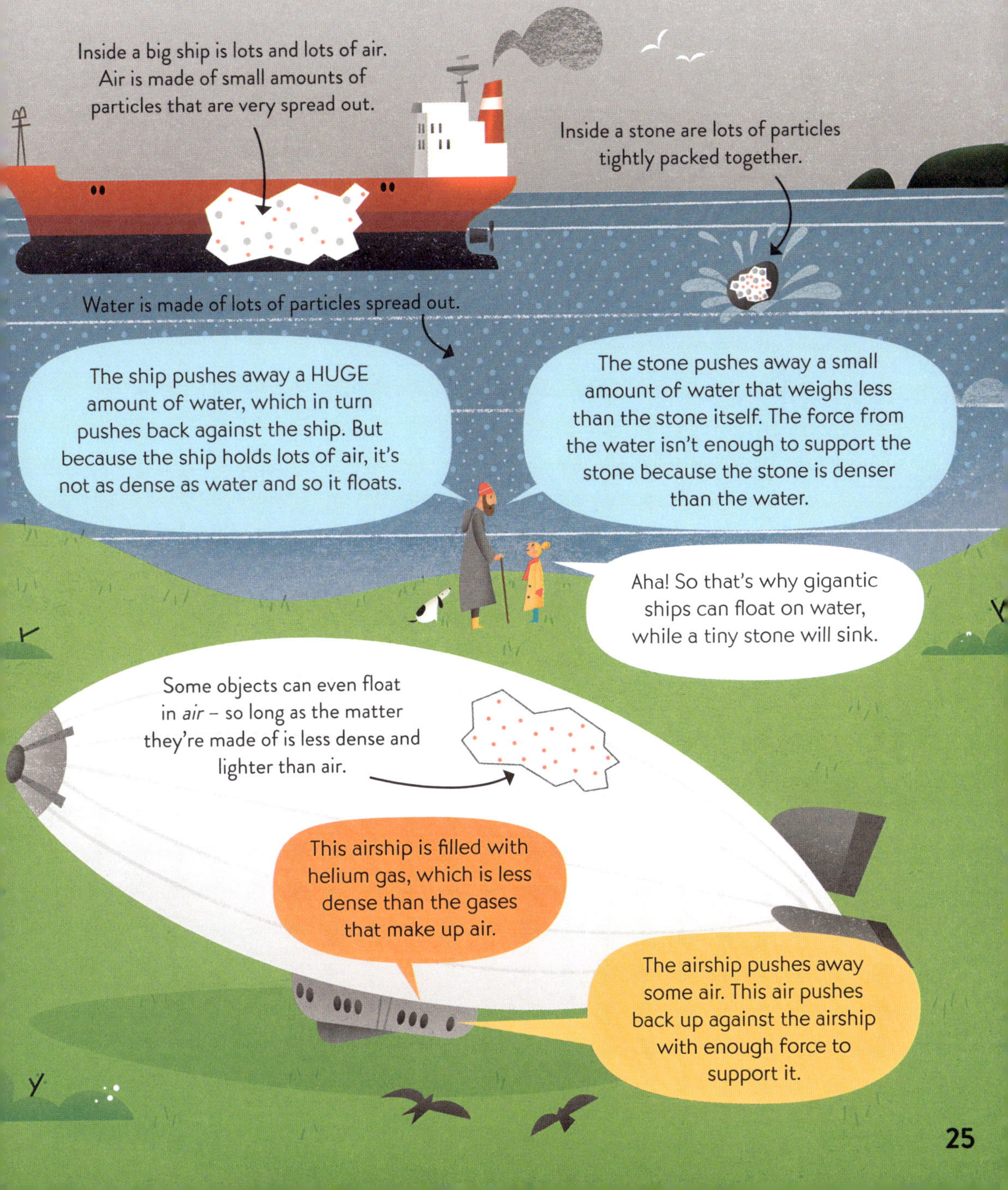

Inside a big ship is lots and lots of air. Air is made of small amounts of particles that are very spread out.
Inside a stone are lots of particles tightly packed together.
Water is made of lots of particles spread out.
The ship pushes away a HUGE amount of water, which in turn pushes back against the ship. But because the ship holds lots of air, it's not as dense as water and so it floats.
The stone pushes away a small amount of water that weighs less than the stone itself. The force from the water isn't enough to support the stone because the stone is denser than the water.
Aha! So that's why gigantic ships can float on water, while a tiny stone will sink.
Some objects can even float in *air* – so long as the matter they're made of is less dense and lighter than air.
This airship is filled with helium gas, which is less dense than the gases that make up air.
The airship pushes away some air. This air pushes back up against the airship with enough force to support it.

Friction

When things rub up against each other, it creates the force of **friction**. It's what makes a ball slow down and come to a stop even when it rolls across a flat surface. Friction slows objects moving through air and water, too, because they brush up against the particles that make up those things.

To go fast, athletes do all they can to reduce friction. A smooth shape reduces friction, so...

Splash!
...I shave all my body hair to make myself more sleek.
...I wear a swimsuit made of a smooth, tight fabric.
...I wear a cap and goggles with smooth surfaces.
...the way I'm swimming makes a long, slim *streamlined* shape.

Animals need to reduce friction, too. For example, birds of prey form streamlined shapes as they fly, so they can dive as fast as possible to catch their food.

Some things work better with *more* friction. Footwear and tires on vehicles, for instance, are covered in bumps and have rough surfaces. These increase grip and prevent slipping.

Speed and energy

It's the speed that really counts in kinetic energy. A car driving at 37mph, for instance, has *four times* the kinetic energy of a car driving at 18mph – and the potential for four times more destruction in a crash.

20

SCREECH

Escaping Earth

Speed is also crucial in creating enough energy to launch a rocket into space. To escape the Earth's massive gravitational pull, a rocket needs to reach a take-off speed of 25,000mph – 120 times the take-off speed of a passenger plane. It also needs to carry enough fuel to power lift-off.

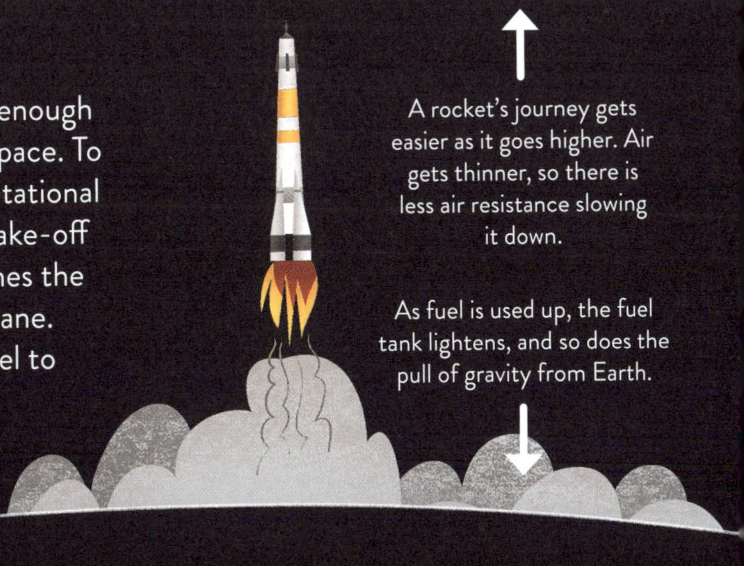
A rocket's journey gets easier as it goes higher. Air gets thinner, so there is less air resistance slowing it down.
As fuel is used up, the fuel tank lightens, and so does the pull of gravity from Earth.

A rocket's heaviest load is fuel. The challenge for scientists is to keep the rocket's weight as low as possible. In the future, it may be possible to power rockets by manipulating forces in new ways...

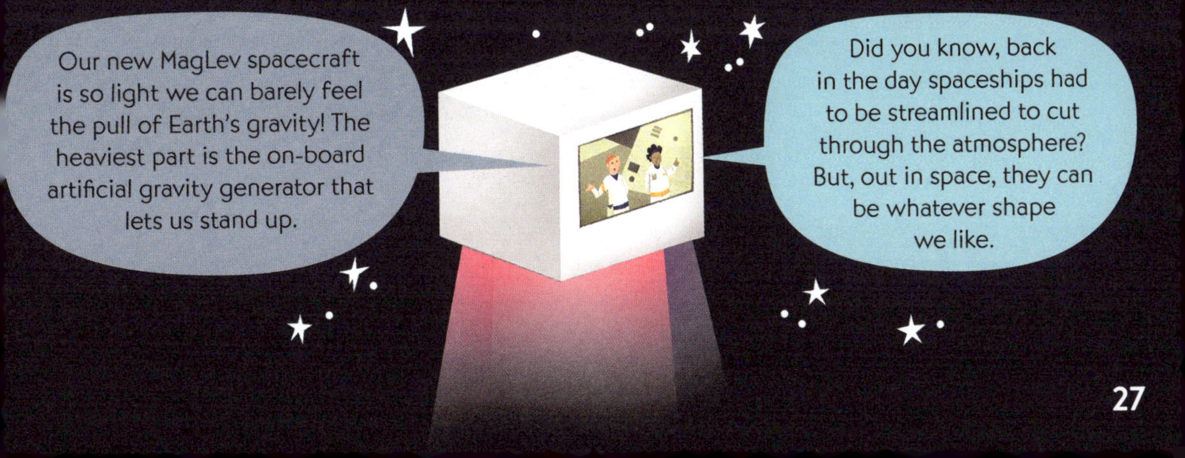
Our new MagLev spacecraft is so light we can barely feel the pull of Earth's gravity! The heaviest part is the on-board artificial gravity generator that lets us stand up.
Did you know, back in the day spaceships had to be streamlined to cut through the atmosphere? But, out in space, they can be whatever shape we like.

Why does my hair stick to this balloon?

How do waves carry messages through space?

How is a ripple on a pond like a beam of light?

Chapter 2
WAVES

Waves are everywhere. Waves rise and fall in the ocean, and earthquakes create tremors that spread in waves through the ground. As you turn the pages of this book, light waves are bouncing off the words and sound waves are pulsing through the air and into your ears.

And there are many more kinds of waves you can't see or hear, including radio waves, infrared waves and ultraviolet waves.

Physicists are fascinated by how waves move and change as they interact with the world. Studying them has led to incredible inventions – from television and Wi-Fi to night-vision cameras and treatments for cancer.

What are waves?

All waves are forms of **vibrations** that carry energy. Some waves are fast; some are slow. Some form big, stretched-out shapes; others make small, tight ones. As waves move, they come across things in their path, and react with them in different ways.

Here's one kind of wave...

...an ocean wave, approaching a surfer.
Huh. That's only a little wave.
As the wave passes under the surfer, she bobs up.
Here comes a big wave at last!
As the wave passes, the surfer bobs down again.

As ocean waves move *horizontally* to the shore, the surfer moves *vertically*. After each wave passes, the surfer is more or less back to where she started.

Here's another kind of wave...

I can make the coils of this spring move back and forth in waves.
?
Slink
Doiiing
Doiiing
Oh, I see what you mean now.

Waves passing through a coiled spring move in a different way. As one person pushes against one end of the spring, the coils move and bounce against each other, causing a wave that travels through the spring. The coils move in the *same direction* as the wave but don't stay in the same place like the surfer on her board.

Describing a wave

Physicists can figure out a huge amount about waves and how they behave by examining their shape, and timing their motion. Imagine a person is standing in a lake and throwing a stone into the water. Ripples – which are a kind of wave – travel across the water until they hit the person's legs.

SPLASH

Each ripple is the top half of a wave.

The distance between the ripples is called the **wavelength.**

The number of ripples that hit my legs every second is called the **frequency**.

The height of the ripple is called the **amplitude.**

A shorter wavelength creates more ripples per second – so these waves have a *higher* frequency.

When the waves hit me, they bounce off at an angle.

A longer wavelength creates fewer ripples per second, so has a *lower* frequency.

It's not just waves in *water* that bounce off things and change direction. It's true for many kinds of waves, including **light** and **sound waves**. By studying and measuring easily visible ripples, physicists have been able to work out a lot about how these other, often *invisible*, waves work.

Sound waves

Sound waves are made by vibrations – in air, liquids or even solid objects. All three are made up of **particles**, and it's these particles that push against each other, creating a wave that moves a little like the coils in a spring. If that wave of vibrations reaches your ear, you'll detect it as a sound.

The **pitch**, which describes how high or low a sound is, depends on the wave's frequency, and on how compact or spread out the wave is as it moves.

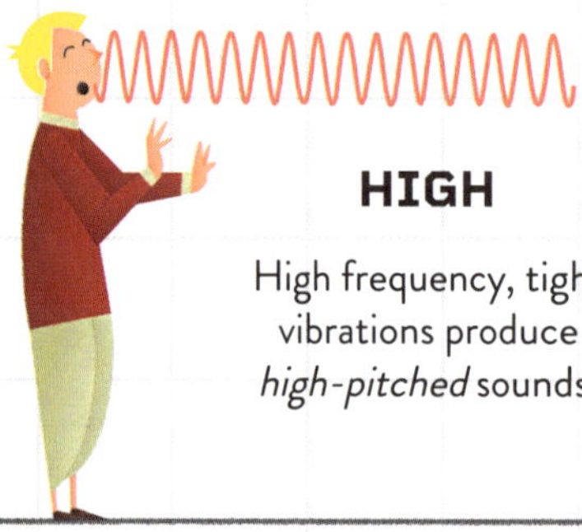

HIGH

High frequency, tight vibrations produce *high-pitched* sounds.

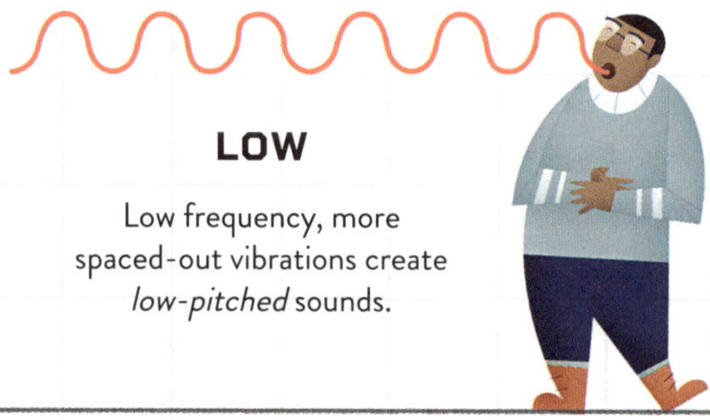

LOW

Low frequency, more spaced-out vibrations create *low-pitched* sounds.

Louder sounds create bigger vibrations with waves that have a big amplitude.

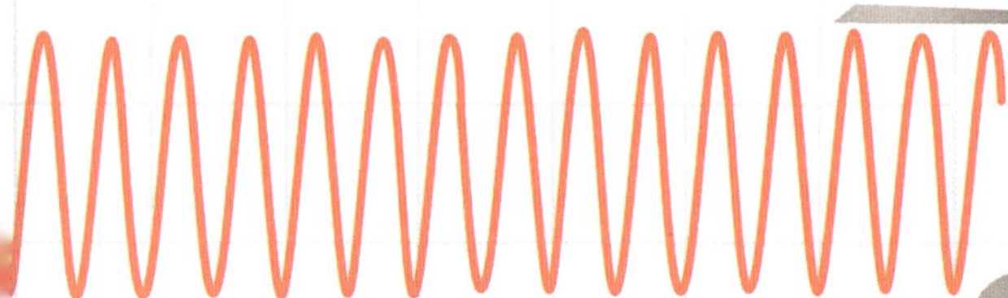

LOUD

Some sounds are so loud they can damage your hearing. So people have to wear protection on their ears when they are near.

SOFT

Softer sounds create smaller vibrations with little amplitude waves.

Changing sound

Have you ever noticed how the siren of an *approaching* emergency vehicle changes in tone as it passes and *moves away*? That's due to something called the **doppler effect**. It happens when sound waves get bunched together then spread out again.

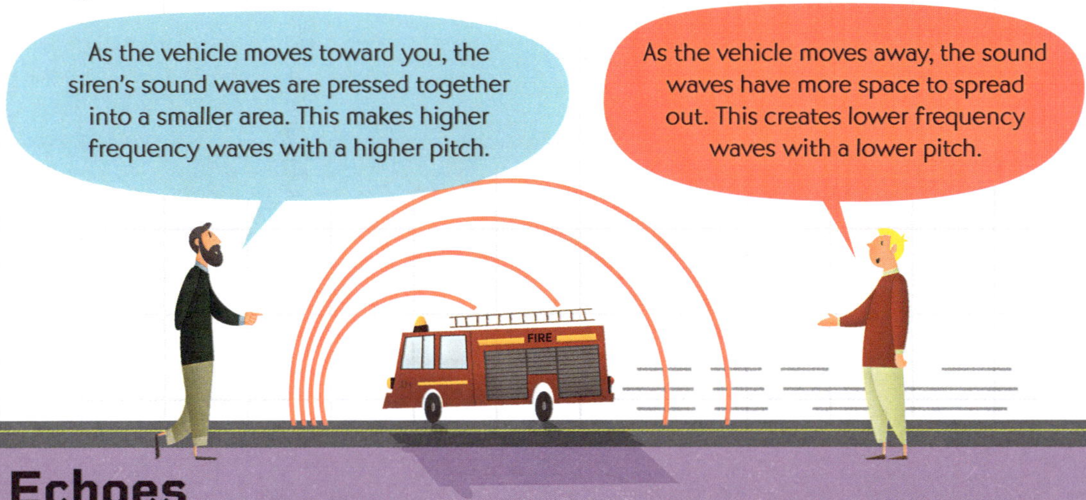
As the vehicle moves toward you, the siren's sound waves are pressed together into a smaller area. This makes higher frequency waves with a higher pitch.
As the vehicle moves away, the sound waves have more space to spread out. This creates lower frequency waves with a lower pitch.
FIRE

Echoes

Sound waves *reflect* off surfaces, just like waves of water. You can tell that sound is reflecting when you hear an **echo**. Empty rooms with hard smooth surfaces for sound to bounce off of produce lots of echoes. Rooms full of furniture, drapes and carpets absorb the sound, so produce little echo.

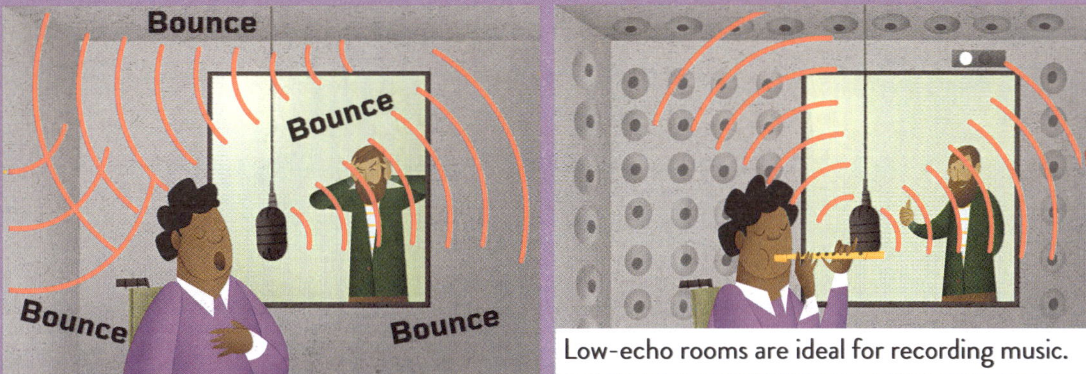
Bounce
Bounce
Bounce
Bounce

Low-echo rooms are ideal for recording music.

Moving through space

Sound waves *can't travel* through empty space, because there are no particles to vibrate. But other waves, such as **light waves**, can. That's because light is made from vibrating electric and magnetic fields that don't require moving particles. To explain this, we need to talk about electricity, and tiny particles called electrons.

Turn the page to find out more...

Electrons and electric charge

Every object is made up of tiny parts called atoms. And inside are even *tinier* parts – or *particles* – including **electrons.** These move around the edge of the atom. It's electrons that cause electricity.

Electrons orbit around the core – the **nucleus** – of an atom. Each electron has what's called a **negative charge**, often shown like this:

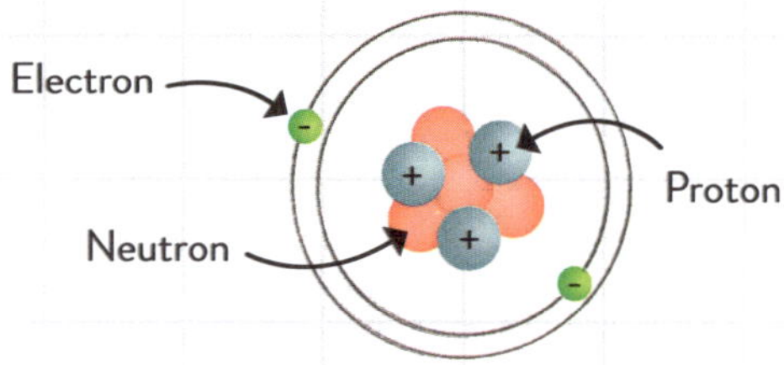

Electron
Neutron
Proton

Inside the nucleus are particles called protons and neutrons. Neutrons have no charge; protons have a **positive charge**, shown like this:

When atoms have the same number of electrons and protons, the charges cancel each other out. But, sometimes, electrons jump from one thing to another. If something *gains* electrons it becomes *negatively* charged. If it *loses* electrons it becomes *positively* charged. And here's what's important: **opposite charges attract.**

Sticky electricity

You can create a pair of opposite charges surprisingly easily. You just have to rub your hair with a balloon.

When the balloon rubs against my head, electrons jump from the hairs onto the balloon.
My hair loses electrons, and becomes positively charged.
The balloon gains electrons from the hairs and becomes negatively charged.
Positive and negative charges attract each other...
...so the hairs stick to the balloon.

This type of charge is known as **static electricity.** You may even see an electric spark and hear a crackle in the air. That's the electrons from your hair colliding rapidly with atoms in the air on their way to the balloon.

Electric fields

Rubbing your hair with a balloon creates an electric charge in the balloon and on your hair. It also means that there's something called an **electric field** around both. This an invisible force that affects things that enter the field.

Imagine charging up a metal ball so that it loses electrons. It'll end up with a positive electric field around it.

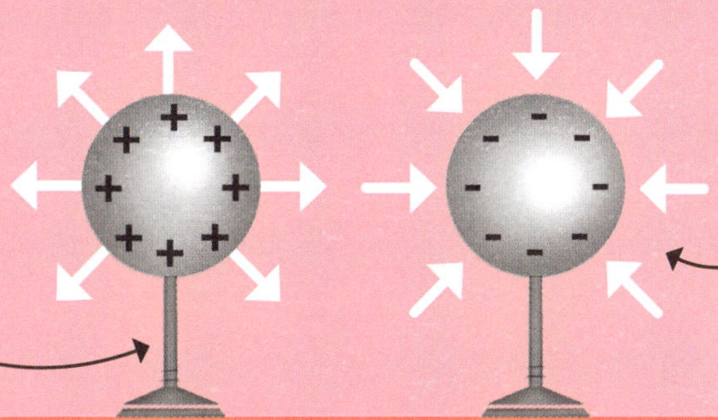

Or, you could give it a negative charge. This time, its electric field will act in the opposite direction.

Magnetic fields

The rule that "opposite charges attract" isn't just true for electric fields. It's also true for **magnetic fields** – fields that exist around magnets. It's what makes magnets stick to certain metals, such as iron or nickel. You can't *see* a magnetic field. But you can see the *effects*, when other magnets or metals come near.

If you could see the magnetic field around a magnet, it'd look like this:

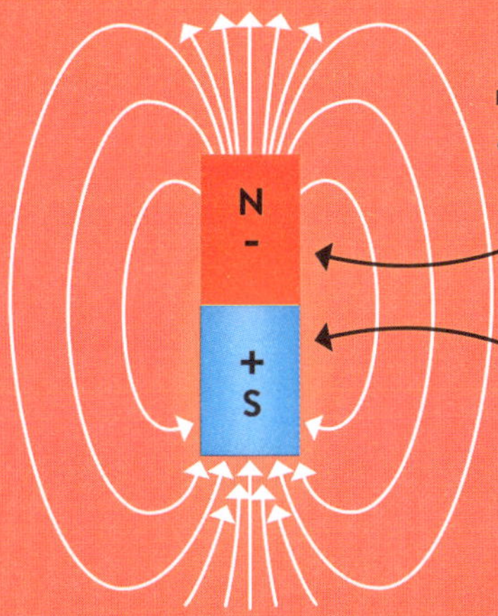

One end of the magnet is negative and is known as its north pole.

The other end is positive and is known as its south pole.

The north pole of one magnet is attracted to the south pole of another, making it hard to pull them apart.

It's also an effort to make the matching poles of two magnets come together.

Magnets work because of the way their electrons move. There are different types of magnets. Some are permanent, some are temporary and some can be switched on and off. Turn the page to find out more...

Electromagnetism

Here's a key physics fact: a moving or changing magnetic field can generate a flow of electrons – creating something called an **electric current**. This discovery, by Danish scientist Hans Christian Ørsted, got English physicist Michael Faraday very curious. He experimented to find out what was going on.

When I pass an electric current along this wire, it creates a weak magnetic field.
I can make the field stronger if I bend the wire into coils.
When the current is on, any iron object that's near enough will be attracted to this device.

These kinds of devices are called **electromagnets**. Today, they make all sorts of things *work*, from motors to loudspeakers to doorbells. The advantage of electromagnets is they can make a machine stop and start with the flick of a switch.

How a doorbell works

When you press an electric doorbell, electric current flows through an electromagnet. This creates a magnetic force of attraction that draws a permanent magnet with a clapper attached to hit a bell. Here's a diagram to explain.

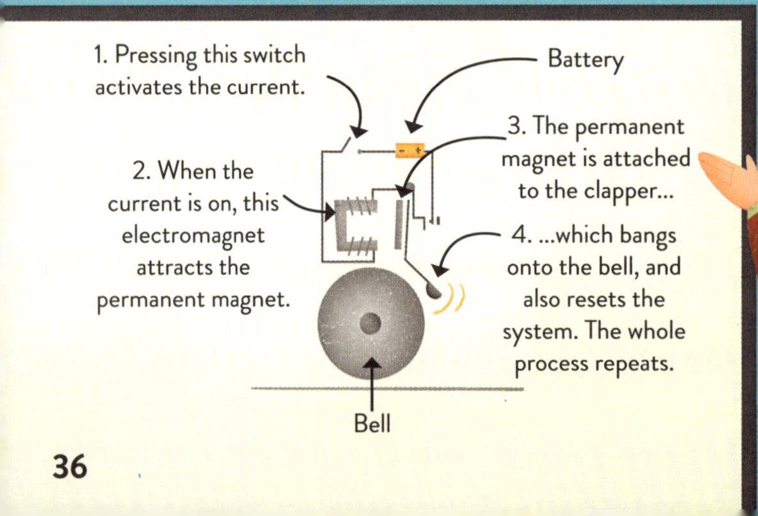
1. Pressing this switch activates the current.
Battery
2. When the current is on, this electromagnet attracts the permanent magnet.
3. The permanent magnet is attached to the clapper...
4. ...which bangs onto the bell, and also resets the system. The whole process repeats.
Bell

And now you know all this, let's get back to waves!

Electromagnetic waves and light

Here's another physics fact: a moving charged particle – such as an atom with excess electrons – produces electric *and* magnetic fields that travel as waves moving at the speed of light. In other words, light and electricity and magnetism are all related. This was discovered by James Clerk Maxwell in the 1860s.

I will call these moving electric and magnetic fields **electromagnetic waves.**

Here are three important things to know about electromagnetic waves:

1. They can travel through empty space – including outer space.

2. They include a kind of wave you can see – it's called **visible light**.

3. They carry energy and behave, more or less, like other kinds of waves, such as waves in water. This means it's possible to measure their *frequency* and *wavelength.*

The spectrum of light

In fact, electromganetic waves travel in a range of wavelengths – from very long, low energy ones to very short, high energy ones. And they can all be measured. This range is known as the **electromagnetic specturm**.

The waves with the longest wavelengths and lowest energy and frequency in the spectrum are called **radio waves.**

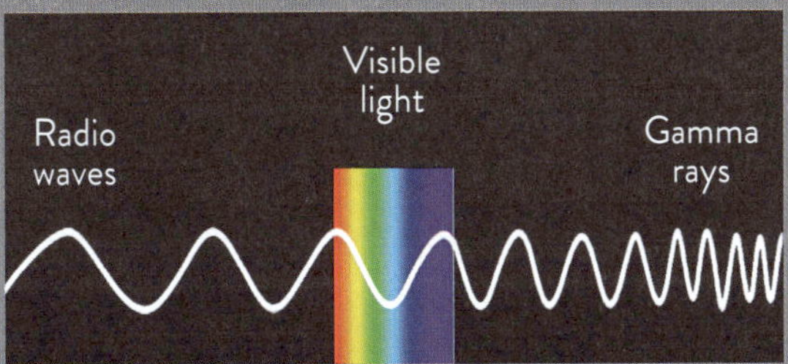
Radio waves
Visible light
Gamma rays

The waves with the smallest wavelengths and highest energy and frequency are called **gamma rays.**

Visible light is made up of medium-sized wavelengths, in the middle of the spectrum.

What's fascinating is how these different kinds of waves behave when they meet things in their path, and how people can use them. Turn the page to find out about some of them, and how they have transformed our lives...

Radio waves

Radio waves can travel easily over long distances, through buildings, water, trees, the Earth's atmosphere and into space. They can even bend around mountains without being absorbed or lost.

Hi folks, you are receiving this LIVE broadcast of a concert using radio waves. The waves travel to a transmission tower and then to a receiver in your home.

Microwaves

Microwaves pass through glass, ceramics and plastic, but are absorbed by water. This is what makes microwave ovens work.

Microwaves make the water molecules in food vibrate. This heats up the food.
Ding
Cell phones, satellite broadcasting and Wi-Fi send signals using microwaves.
Microwave signals don't travel easily over hills and underground, which is why signals are often poor in hilly areas or basements.

Infrared

Objects emit infrared light waves as heat. They're invisible to humans but some animals use them to spot prey at night.

Infrared is used in TV remote controls, security sensors and night vision cameras.

I can spot wildlife at night using a heat vision camera that detects heat or infrared light waves emitted from these deer.

Visible light

Visible light is one small range of wavelengths in the middle of the spectrum. Either side, wavelengths are too big or too small to be detected by human eyes. Visible light takes on different qualities – or colors – depending on the size of its wavelengths. We usually see the colors together as white light, but this can be separated into the colors of the rainbow, like the one on page 12, when using a **prism**...

Ultraviolet light

Humans can't see ultraviolet (or UV) light, but bees can. They use it to find nectar in flowers. Humans have built machines that copy this ability – to detect ultraviolet ink on paper money.

Aha, no UV ink here. It's a forgery!

Ultraviolet light can damage human cells.
But it can be used for good, to break down viruses and bacteria in hospitals.

X-rays

X-rays can travel through most materials except bone or metal. This makes them useful for seeing inside things.

Ah, that bone is definitely broken. We'll have to operate.

I'm sorry, you can't bring your scissors on the airplane.

Gamma rays

Gamma rays are incredibly powerful and can travel through many materials, unless they are very dense.

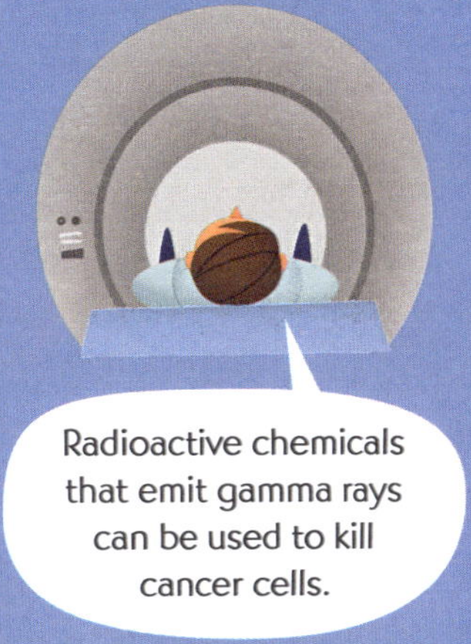
Radioactive chemicals that emit gamma rays can be used to kill cancer cells.

Gamma ray machines can zap bacteria and viruses in food, prevent fungus growth and stop fruit from ripening too fast.

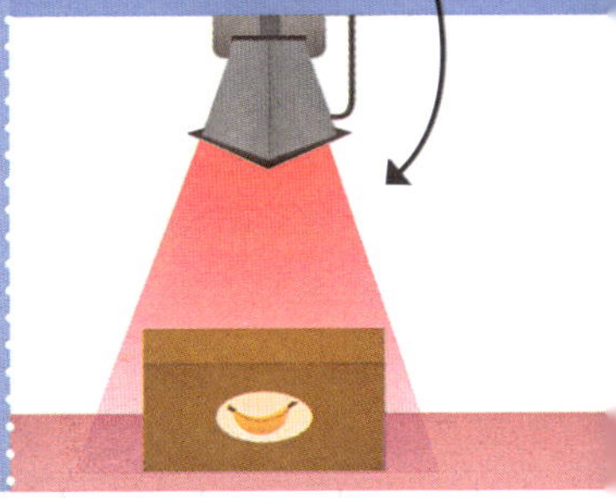

Prisms, like the one I'm holding, bend light as it travels through. Each wavelength of light bends by a different amount, separating white light into bands of colors.
Violet light has the shortest wavelength and bends the most.
Newton

Peering into space and time

Physicists are developing more and more complex equipment to detect electromagnetic waves in space. With these, they hope to find out about things, not just in our galaxy, but REALLY FAR AWAY, too.

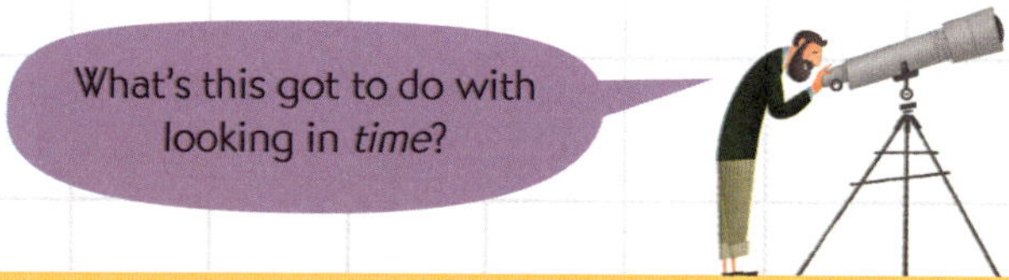
What's this got to do with looking in *time*?

When you look through a standard telescope at the Moon, you see the Moon as it was 1.3 seconds ago in the past. That's because it takes 1.3 seconds for light waves from the Moon to reach your eyes.

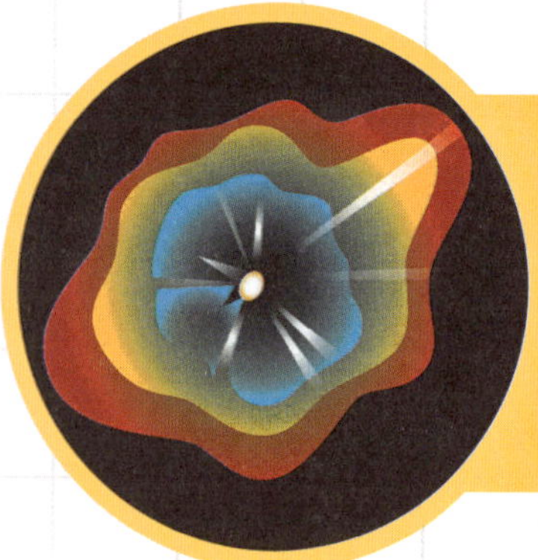

The further away an object is, the longer it takes for light waves from it to reach Earth. So when you look at a spectacular but short-lived event such as a **supernova**, you see it as it was HUNDREDS of years ago. That's because it takes that long for light to reach your eyes.

Now imagine you are using a powerful telescope on a spacecraft above the Earth's atmosphere. This telescope is able to detect gamma rays produced by violent explosions in distant galaxies of the universe.

This telescope can detect things SO FAR AWAY, it picks up events that took place MILLIONS, or even BILLIONS, of years ago.

To look as far as possible into space, scientists have set up giant receiver dishes that pick up unidentified radio waves. These waves have the farthest reach, and are the best chance we have of finding intelligent alien life.

Waves in the future

The remarkable thing about waves is the energy they carry, which enables them to send information across space and travel *through* matter. But they can also damage and destroy things. Physicists are looking at new, safer ways to harness the power of waves, improve lives and protect the planet.

Scientists are experimenting with a new group of waves, previously overlooked, known as Terahertz waves. These lie between microwaves and infrared light on the spectrum.

Terahertz waves penetrate many materials. But unlike ultraviolet light, gamma and X-rays, they don't cause damage to human tissue.
They could be used to detect skin cancer safely, without causing harm.
The beauty of Terahertz waves is that they can be emitted from a tiny microchip.
Small, portable machines with these chips could be used for security or customs, to see inside envelopes and boxes.
Very low frequency waves, such as radio waves...
...can block out harmful radiation released by solar flares.
Did you know, radio waves are rather powerful. They can deflect charged particles from space.
I did know! In fact, humans have already emitted enough radio waves to form a bubble around Earth. It protects us from particles that can be harmful.

Does time pass at the same speed for everyone in the universe?

What does $E = mc^2$ mean?

Where does gravity come from?

Why is Einstein so famous?

Chapter 3

THE SPEED OF LIGHT AND THE SHAPE OF THE UNIVERSE

Some of the greatest leaps forward in how we understand the universe have come from physicists using their imaginations. They used a technique called a **thought experiment**.

Albert Einstein – one of the most famous physicists of all time – often performed thought experiments. One in particular was to do with the speed of light. It led to a scientific revolution in the early 20th century, and changed the way people thought about two seemingly simple ideas: time and distance.

In turn, it led Einstein to rethink the whole universe…

Can light move faster than itself?

Einstein had read that light always moves at a constant speed in empty space. That speed was VERY fast – but people were able to measure it by looking at the movements of planets and stars. He wondered what this fact about light might mean for how we think about movement.

Imagine I'm standing on a train platform, as a train goes by at a constant speed.

As the train goes by...
...the front and the back are struck by lightning.
From where I'm standing, the light travels the same distance to reach me. It looks as if both strikes hit the train at the same time.
So far, straightforward.
But from *my* point of view the flash of the lightning appears to hit the front first.
That's because the passenger is moving forwards, so the light from the back has farther to travel to reach her eyes.
If she was going to see the two strikes hitting at the same time, the light from the back strike would have to travel *faster* than the speed of light – but light *cannot* go faster.

So which one of us is right? Could it be that we're *both* right?
If the speed of light CAN'T change, then *something else* has to – the passing of time, and the distance the light travels.

If the train is going at 125mph, we wouldn't notice that time is moving at a different rate on board.
But, at MUCH faster speeds, say, close to the speed of light, then the slowing of time would be *very* noticeable.
WHOOSH
My calculations show that time and distance are **RELATIVE**. What I can see and measure *standing still*, is different from what a *moving* person can see and measure.
Even if I could fly close to the speed of light for, say, ten minutes, a person watching me would experience this as lasting for *more than* ten minutes.
ZOOOM
Light
That's because we're measuring the same *speed*, but experiencing *time* at different rates.
She'd also see me moving across a shorter amount of space than I would see myself moving, because *space* can change too.
It's strange – but it's the only way the speed of light can *always* stay the same.

Time and space are two parts of the same fabric of the universe, and that fabric can stretch and shrink, depending on your speed, and your point of view.
Squash
Squash

Einstein called this idea his **theory of Special Relativity**, because it describes how space and time exist *relative* to the speed of light.

Scientists now think of space and time as one thing, which they call **spacetime.**

It might sound ridiculous – but that's because it only becomes obvious at INCREDIBLY high speeds or MASSIVE distances. Physicists have proved the theory using many observations. Turn the page to read about just one of these.

How can you measure a muon?

MUONS are tiny particles, smaller than atoms. They're created when high energy protons from the Sun crash into Earth's air. Muons rain down through the atmosphere at close to the speed of light. They travel so fast that we shouldn't be able to detect them at all. But we *can*...

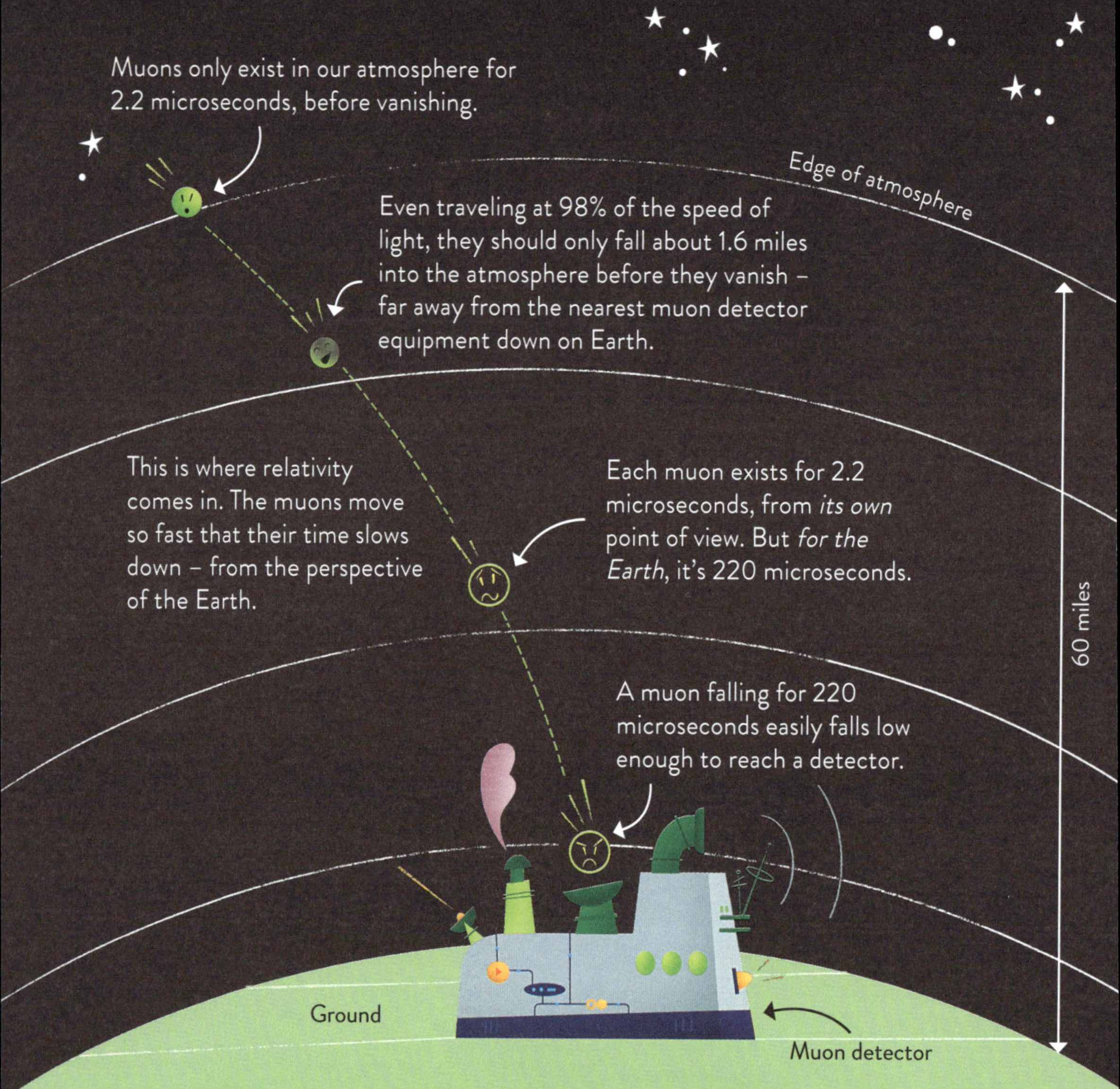

Muons only exist in our atmosphere for 2.2 microseconds, before vanishing.
Edge of atmosphere
Even traveling at 98% of the speed of light, they should only fall about 1.6 miles into the atmosphere before they vanish – far away from the nearest muon detector equipment down on Earth.
This is where relativity comes in. The muons move so fast that their time slows down – from the perspective of the Earth.
Each muon exists for 2.2 microseconds, from *its own* point of view. But *for the Earth*, it's 220 microseconds.
60 miles
A muon falling for 220 microseconds easily falls low enough to reach a detector.
Ground
Muon detector

Finding and analyzing muons takes a lot of special equipment, and quite a bit of math. Because we don't have the experience of things moving at light speed, getting your head around the theory of special relativity can be tricky. But it DOES work.

The trouble with time travel

Physicists, and science fiction authors, have come up with all sorts of thought experiments to demonstrate the effects of special relativity. One in particular had some serious consequences for their ideas of space travel.

Meet identical twins Jess and Tess.
I'm an astronaut, and I'm about to go to space in a new ship that can travel at close to the speed of light.
I'm not going to do that. It sounds really dangerous.
It's a 10 year mission. I can't wait!
10 years?! I'd be so bored.
Jess speeds off in her ship.
Wow, this is FAST.
On board her ship, Tess accelerates to 95% of the speed of light.
10 years go by, according to her on-board clock.
Jan 10 2031
I'll be home soon! Everyone's going to be so excited when I tell them about the amazing things I've seen.
Back on Earth, Tess is waiting to greet her sister.
Tess was going so fast, she experienced time at a different rate from me. She may only have lived through 10 years on her ship...
...but for us on Earth, 38 years have passed.
You look old.
Yup. I AM old.

Right now, humans can't travel anywhere near **lightspeed**. So this kind of slowing of time isn't a serious problem for today's astronauts. But if we ever work out how to travel fast enough to visit other stars, it might be.

Relativity and $E=mc^2$

Einstein's theory of Special Relativity contains one of the most famous bits of mathematics in all of science – the equation $E=mc^2$. But what does it actually *mean*?

E stands for *energy*
m stands for *mass*: the amount of matter an object contains.
$E=mc^2$
c stands for *celerity* – Latin for "speed," and physics code for "the speed of light." That is 983,571,056 feet per second (299,792,458 meters per second).
The **energy** in an object (E) is equal to its **mass** (m) multiplied by the **speed of light** (c) squared. Squared means "multiplied by itself."
Does it mean energy can turn into mass... and that mass contains energy?
That's right.
And there's more. Einstein's equations tell us exactly how much energy any amount of mass contains.
This rock has a mass of 2kg (4.5lbs). So, to figure out how much energy it contains, I have to... multiply 2 by the speed of light squared?
Correct. That rock contains 179,751,035,747,363,528 **joules** of energy.
What's a joule?
It's the word physicists use to say how much energy something holds. Here's a more amazing way to think about it – that number of joules is about as MUCH energy as the ENTIRE U.S. uses in one year.
Woah.

What Einstein did next...

The theory of Special Relativity introduced physics to a world where space and time are one and the same – and where both are *changeable*. Einstein himself was surprised by this idea, and wondered what it meant for one of the forces that dominates physics: gravity.

200 years earlier, physicist Isaac Newton described space and time as a stage that everything in the universe *performed on*. They didn't change.

I explained gravity as a mysterious attraction between objects. My mathematics worked well for predicting how gravity affected objects – but it never explained what *caused* it.

However to Einstein, spacetime was more than just a stage. He saw it as one of the actors in the play.

I have an idea – what if the way spacetime can bend and change is what *causes* gravity? What if it's not some strange invisible force... just the shape of the universe itself?
Boiiiing

Einstein called *this* idea his **theory of General Relativity**. Just like Special Relativity, it sounds seriously weird – but experiments by lots of scientists since have backed it up.

Curving the universe

Einstein's idea was that gravity is caused by mass *bending the fabric of spacetime around it*. The more *massive* an object is, the more it *curves* spacetime around it – and the *stronger* its gravity is.

You could think of spacetime as being like a big sheet that fills the entire universe.

If you put a bowling ball on the sheet, the sheet curves under the mass of the ball.
If you roll a marble across the sheet, its path starts to bend as it gets closer to the bowling ball.
What looks like a force attracting the marble to the bowling ball is really just what happens because the sheet is curved.
Einstein Explains!
Press the button to hear him talk.
Imagine the bowling ball is the Sun, and the marble is Earth. Because the Sun is so big, it bends spacetime a lot, giving it a powerful gravity.
Earth has less mass than the Sun, and so a weaker gravity – but enough to keep the moon in orbit around it.
It also explains why things fall to the ground. It's because Earth is *bending* spacetime.
Spacetime is so cool.

Shifting stars

Einstein's set of equations for General Relativity made sense in mathematics. But to be accepted, they had to be able to prove something in the real world.

One of the predictions of General Relativity was that anything truly MASSIVE in space – say, the Sun – bends *light* around itself.

But we can't *see* spacetime, so how do we prove General Relativity?
There's an eclipse of the Sun coming up in a few days.
So?
It means the Moon will block out light from the Sun for a few seconds. Watch...
When the Sun is out, we can't see the stars. But from our night sky maps, we know exactly where they should be.
During an eclipse, though, we CAN see those stars. And we observe that the ones around the Sun have all moved, by a small amount.
Night sky
Day sky (Eclipse)
How did they move?
It's because the light from those stars is being bent around the curved spacetime the Sun has created.

This effect is called **gravitational lensing**. Once again, one of Einstein's theories had been seen in action.

Bending light and slowing time

One of the key ideas of physics is that different theories describing the universe can be combined. This is called **unifying the theories.** The idea is that if they don't work together, then one of them is probably wrong.

Physicists had proved one part of Einstein's theory: that an object's mass would bend light around it. But in order to fit special and general relativity *together*, they had to think about *time* again.

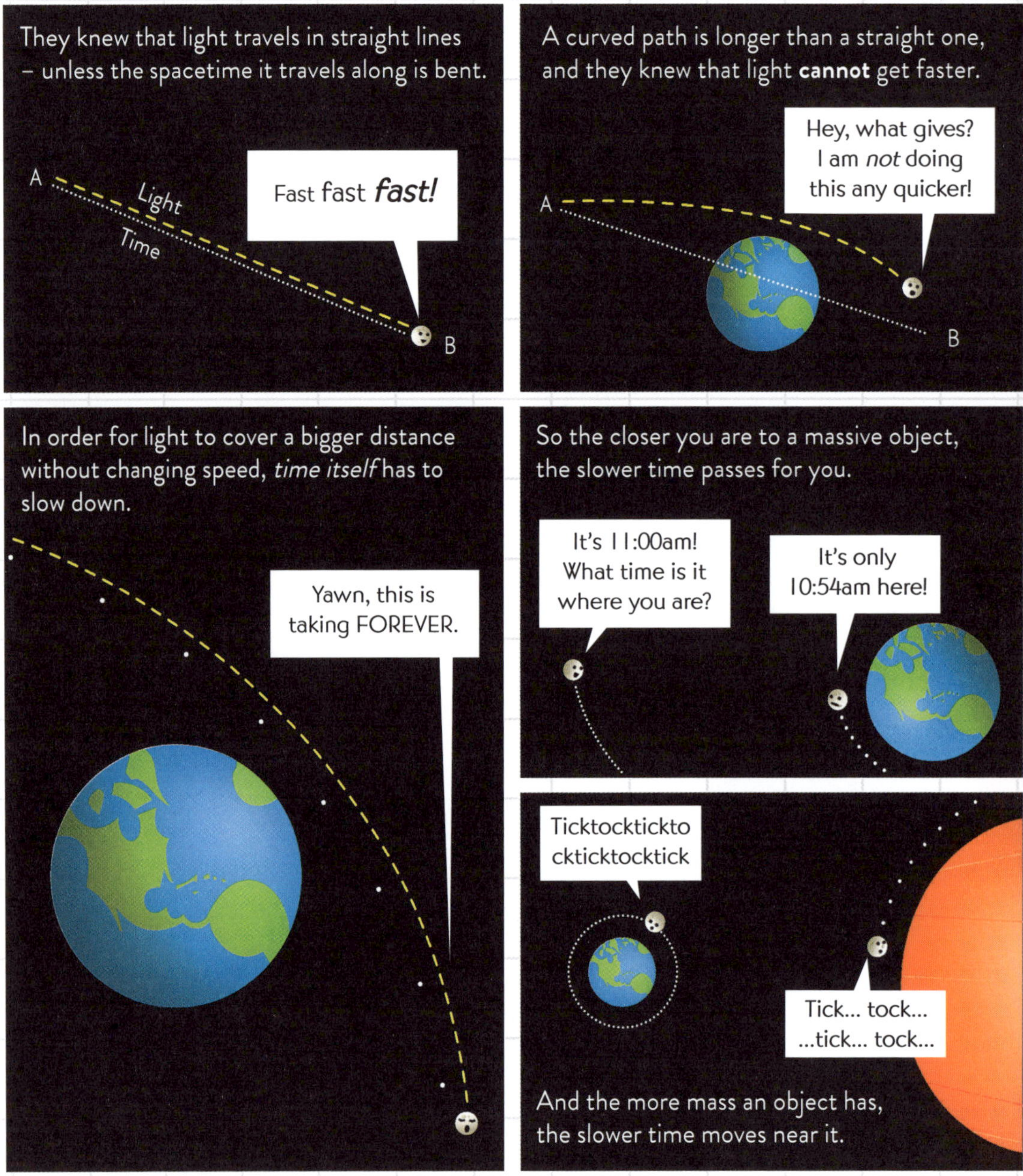
They knew that light travels in straight lines – unless the spacetime it travels along is bent.
A
Light
Time
Fast fast *fast!*
B
A curved path is longer than a straight one, and they knew that light **cannot** get faster.
Hey, what gives? I am *not* doing this any quicker!
A
B
In order for light to cover a bigger distance without changing speed, *time itself* has to slow down.
Yawn, this is taking FOREVER.
So the closer you are to a massive object, the slower time passes for you.
It's 11:00am! What time is it where you are?
It's only 10:54am here!
Ticktocktickto cktickticktock
Tick... tock... ...tick... tock...
And the more mass an object has, the slower time moves near it.

Wait, does that mean time is faster at the top of a tall mountain, because there's less mass up here than down on the ground?
YES – but only by a very *tiny* amount. Not enough to worry about. But higher up, in space, it starts to become a problem.

There's a network of satellites that surrounds Earth known as GPS, which is used to help with navigation. They send information to vehicles on the ground about where they are, and how to find their way on a journey. But, the satellites are *so* high up, they're under less gravity than the computers they're talking to back on Earth.

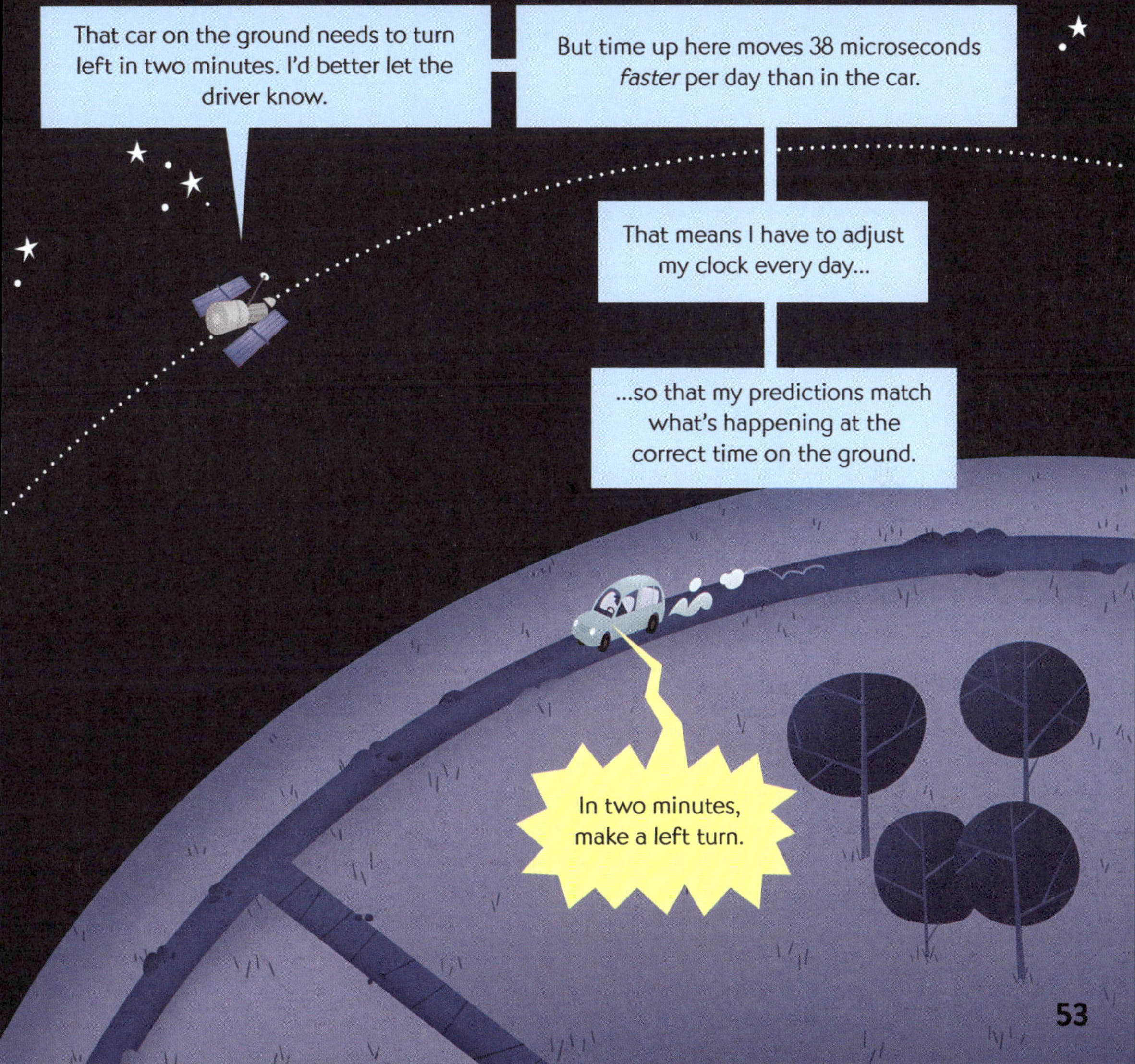
That car on the ground needs to turn left in two minutes. I'd better let the driver know.
But time up here moves 38 microseconds *faster* per day than in the car.
That means I have to adjust my clock every day...
...so that my predictions match what's happening at the correct time on the ground.
In two minutes, make a left turn.

Gravitational waves

One of the predictions of General Relativity is that certain cosmic events send ripples of gravity through spacetime. These are known as **gravitational waves**. They remained just a theory for a hundred years, until an experiment proved General Relativity's predictions correct yet again...

Just like a stone thrown into a lake, something massive happening in deep space should send ripples through spacetime.

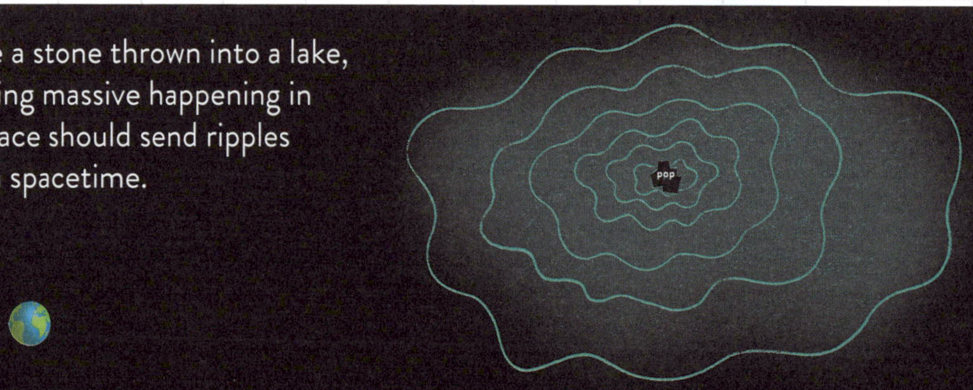
pop

The waves are strongest *near* the event, getting weaker as they radiate out. Detecting them on Earth is difficult, as so far these events have happened VERY far away.

Look here, what kind of events are we talking about?
Well, in theory, any kind of event. But really we're talking about something that will create really STRONG ripples.
How about a supernova, which is the death explosion of a GIGANTIC star? Or perhaps something really difficult to see, such as two black holes colliding.

In 2002, an experiment was set up in the U.S. to detect exactly such a collision, and in particular to see if the resulting gravitational waves could be felt on Earth. Read on to see what the team who ran the experiment discovered.

I'm coming for you.
Bring. It. On.

Spotting spacetime ripples

The experiment relied on a machine called LIGO. Its job was to look for any miniscule changes in spacetime on Earth, specifically those caused by gravitational waves. It does this by measuring the distance between two sets of mirrors.

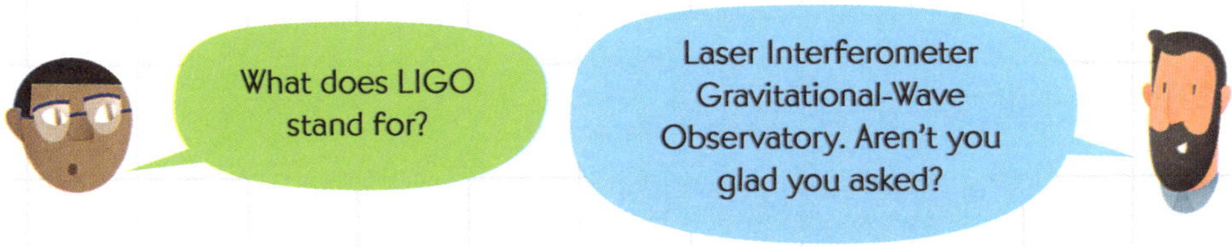

What does LIGO stand for?
Laser Interferometer Gravitational-Wave Observatory. Aren't you glad you asked?

LIGO is made of two arms, each 2.5 miles long, with beams of light running through them. The beams of light measure the distance between two sets of mirrors. If those mirrors move by even the *tiniest* amount, LIGO can detect it.

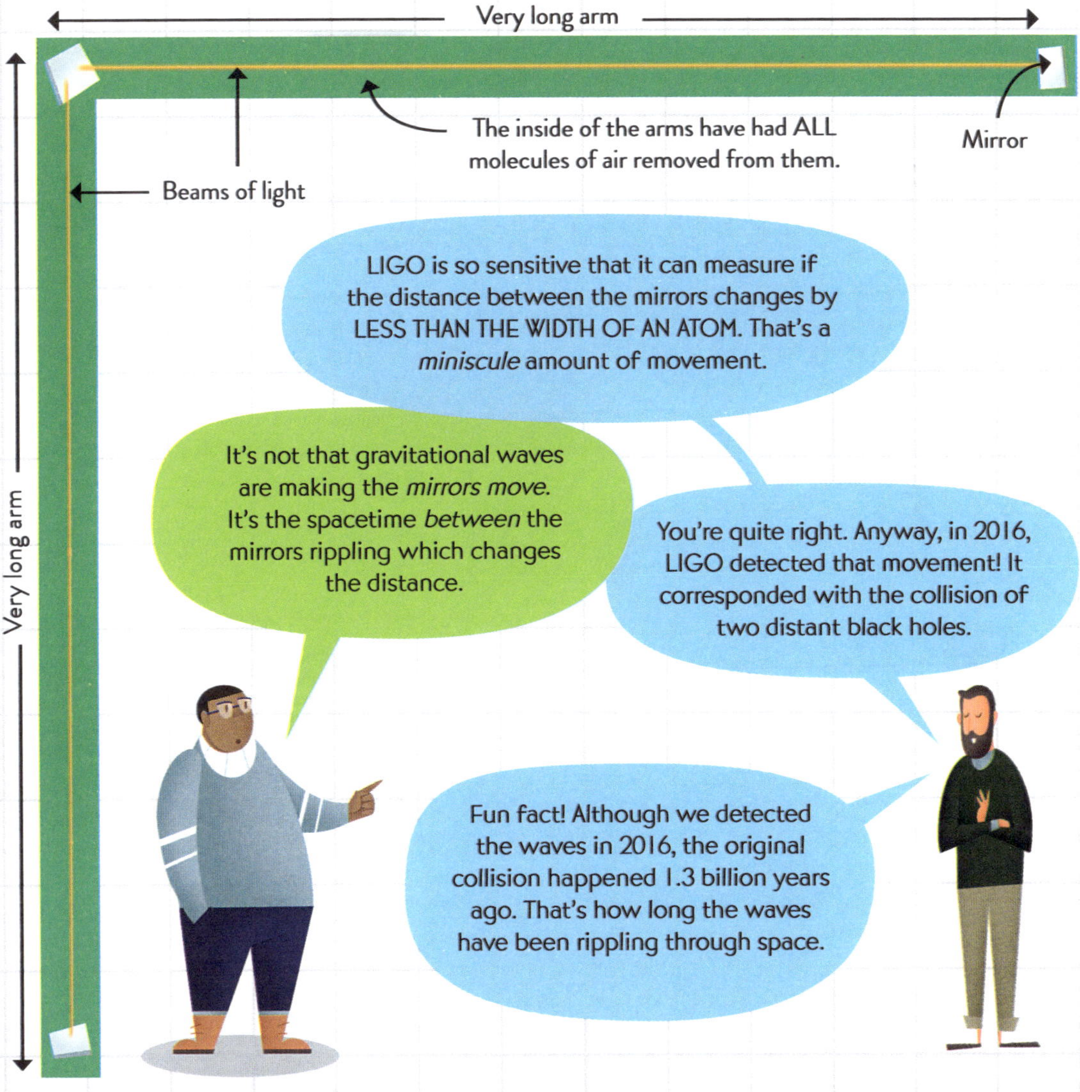

Very long arm
The inside of the arms have had ALL molecules of air removed from them.
Mirror
Beams of light
Very long arm
LIGO is so sensitive that it can measure if the distance between the mirrors changes by LESS THAN THE WIDTH OF AN ATOM. That's a *miniscule* amount of movement.
It's not that gravitational waves are making the *mirrors move*. It's the spacetime *between* the mirrors rippling which changes the distance.
You're quite right. Anyway, in 2016, LIGO detected that movement! It corresponded with the collision of two distant black holes.
Fun fact! Although we detected the waves in 2016, the original collision happened 1.3 billion years ago. That's how long the waves have been rippling through space.

What are atoms made of?

What are the things that *atoms* are made of... made of?

Is nuclear power good or bad?

Why are some things radioactive?

Chapter 4
NUCLEAR & PARTICLE PHYSICS

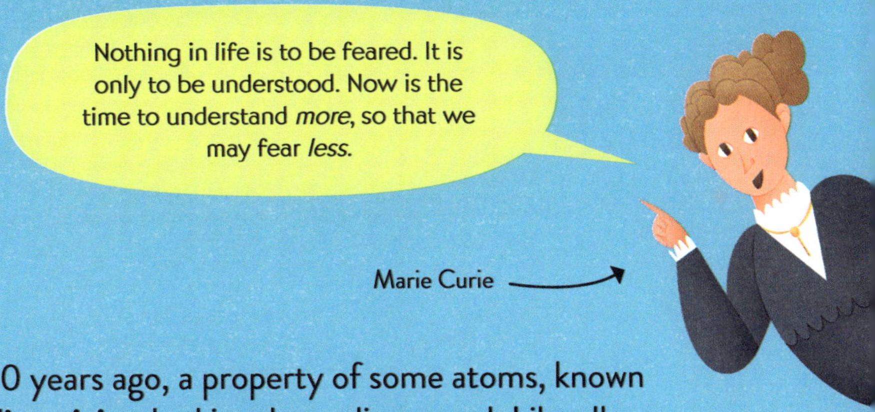
Nothing in life is to be feared. It is only to be understood. Now is the time to understand *more*, so that we may fear *less*.
Marie Curie

Over 100 years ago, a property of some atoms, known as **radioactivity**, had just been discovered. Like all physicists, Marie Curie was deeply curious, and wanted to understand more about why it happens.

Curie and other physicists working at the same time soon found that there was more to atoms than anyone had suspected. They began to uncover the hidden world of the **particles** that made up atoms, and indeed the universe.

The studies of how these atoms and particles interact are known as **nuclear physics** and **particle physics**.

Inside atoms

It's easy to think of atoms as tiny balls that all stick together to make up matter – but it's not quite like that. Atoms come in two parts: an outer part, and an inner area known as the **nucleus**, with a *lot* of empty space in between.

An invisible solar system

An atom's nucleus is made of two types of particles – **protons** and **neutrons**. The nucleus is orbited by other particles called **electrons**, a little like planets orbiting the Sun.

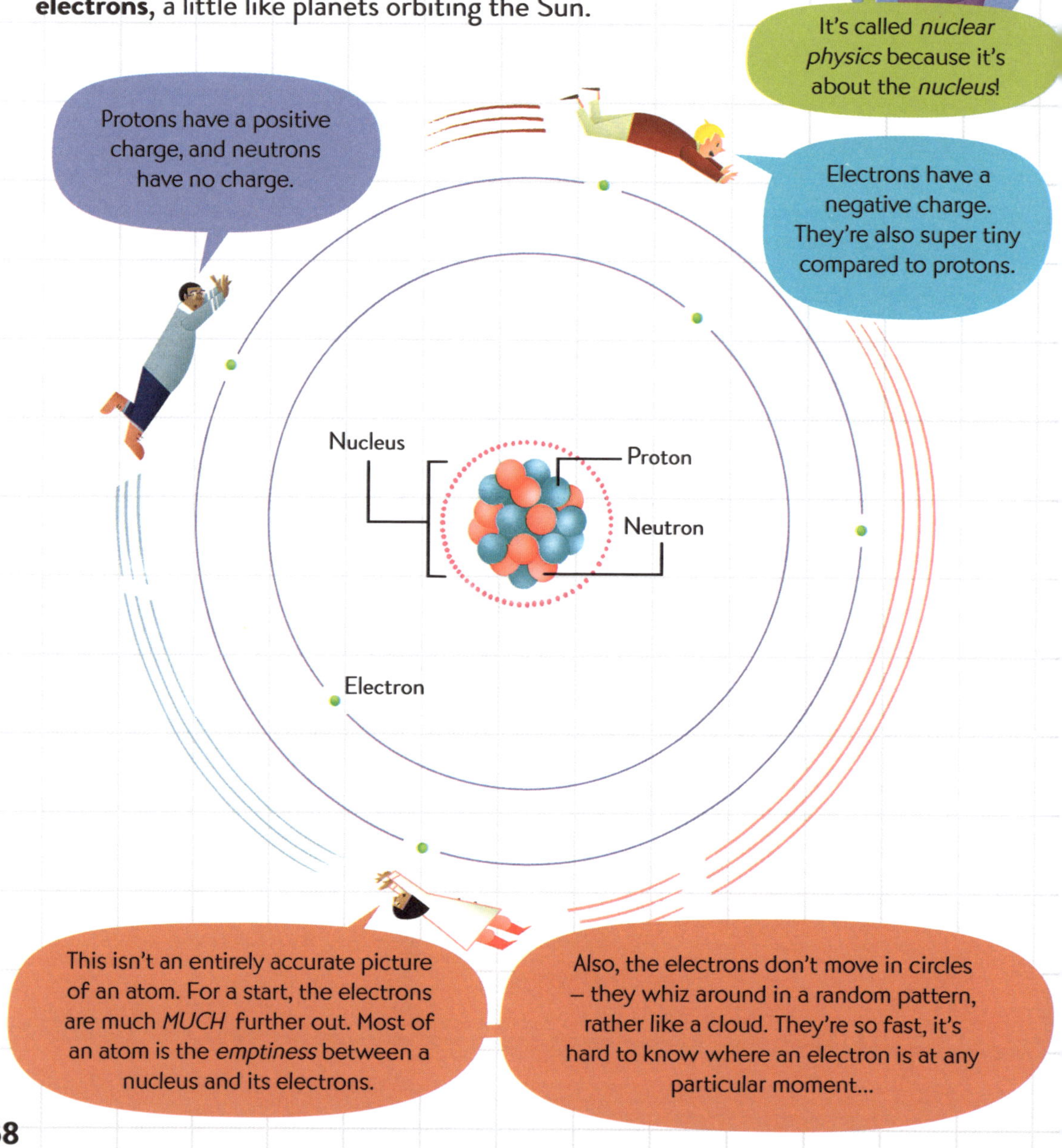
It's called *nuclear physics* because it's about the *nucleus*!
Protons have a positive charge, and neutrons have no charge.
Electrons have a negative charge. They're also super tiny compared to protons.
Nucleus
Proton
Neutron
Electron
This isn't an entirely accurate picture of an atom. For a start, the electrons are much *MUCH* further out. Most of an atom is the *emptiness* between a nucleus and its electrons.
Also, the electrons don't move in circles – they whiz around in a random pattern, rather like a cloud. They're so fast, it's hard to know where an electron is at any particular moment...

The battle of the forces

Unlike planets orbiting the Sun, electrons aren't attracted to the nucleus because of gravity. What causes the *negatively* charged electrons to be attracted to the *positively* charged protons is **electromagnetism**. It should also make all those protons fly apart, because they all have the same charge. But that's where a *new* force comes in – the **strong nuclear force**.

In the everyday world, the electromagnetic force makes sure that things with the same charge are repelled from each other.

Pushing two positive particles together is the same as pushing the positive ends of two magnets together (see page 36).

Hmphhh
Hrrrrr
In other words, it's really difficult!

The strong nuclear force is MUCH more powerful than the electromagnetic force – but it only works over the incredibly short distances found inside the nucleus.

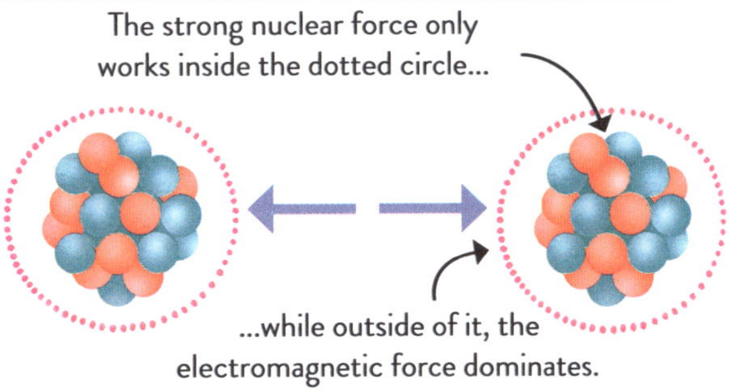
The strong nuclear force only works inside the dotted circle...
...while outside of it, the electromagnetic force dominates.

The electromagnetic force might be weaker, but it extends across the entire universe.

It's as if you had two magnets covered in a very strong glue. It takes a lot of effort to push the same charged ends of the magnets together – but once you do, they stay stuck there.

We can do this! If we just get these magnets to touch, they'll stick together forever!
As they're all positively charged, the electromagnetic force is constantly trying to push the protons apart.
Protons need a *lot* of energy to stay together, but the nucleus of an atom is *packed* with it.
Glue
Glue

Breaking into a nucleus

The strong nuclear force is, well, *strong*. It uses a lot of energy to keep the nucleus of an atom glued together. The nucleus *can* be broken open – releasing staggering amounts of energy, that can be used to power our world – or for destruction. But that process, known as **nuclear fission**, isn't easy.

To start with, you need the right kind of nucleus – an *unstable* one. An unstable nucleus has LOTS of protons and neutrons, so the strong force can't hold it together as well.

To begin the fission process, a single neutron is fired towards an unstable nucleus...

One example of an unstable nucleus is a rare type of metal called **uranium**. Specifically, a version called ^{235}U which is *very* unstable.

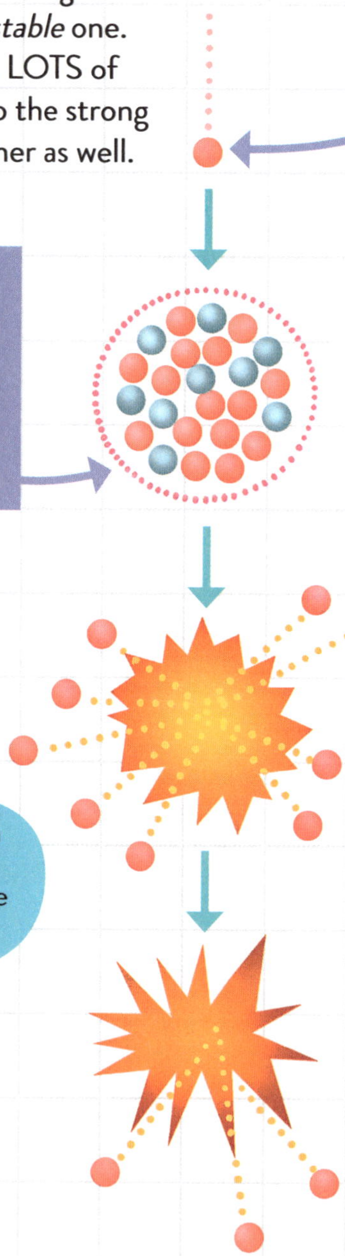

...smashing it open. This releases a lot of energy – as well as very fast-moving neutrons which are shoved out of the nucleus.

These neutrons then smash into *other* unstable atoms, breaking them apart and creating more energy and sending more neutrons flying.

Breaking the nucleus open also produces dangerous **radioactive** particles – more about them in a moment.

This process is called a **chain reaction**. As each atom splits, it helps to split the others around it.

With great power...

Nuclear fission is used in nuclear power stations to generate electricity.

The chain reaction is very carefully controled.

The energy produced is used to boil massive vats of water.

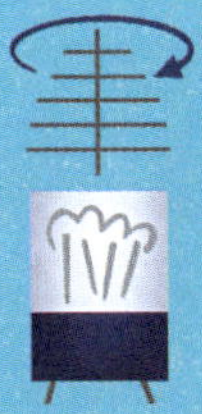

The steam from the boiling water turns turbines, which generate electricity.

Nuclear power doesn't involve burning coal, or oil, which pollute the air...

...but it *does* produce radioactive toxic waste, which is incredibly dangerous. Being near it can cause cancer in people, animals and plants.

Toxic waste has to be stored very carefully – usually in huge drums of steel and concrete. It can stay dangerous for thousands of years.

...comes great responsibility

Unfortunately, nuclear fission can also cause huge amounts of damage.

In the 1980s, a nuclear power station in Chernobyl, Ukraine, went into **meltdown**.

A meltdown is when a chain reaction becomes out of control and the power station is at risk of exploding.

The entire area around the Chernobyl plant had to be evacuated, and remains dangerous to visit to this day.

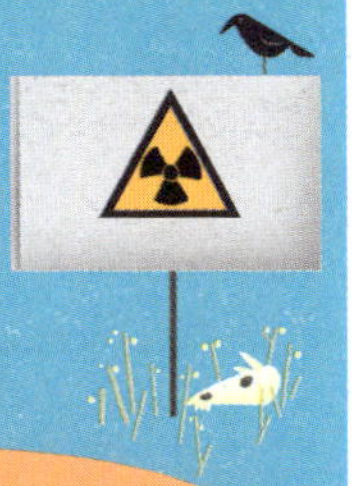

During the 1940s, scientists in the USA developed **atomic bombs** – weapons that use nuclear fission.

Those atomic bombs were used to destroy two cities in Japan, at the end of the Second World War.

Atomic bombs not only cause huge destruction, but also make the air and soil toxic for years afterwards. Many countries have agreed to make their use in wars illegal.

Radioactivity

To stay stable, atoms like to have as little energy as possible. To do this the nucleus needs a *balance* of protons and neutrons. An atom that's out of balance can change by a process known as **radioactive decay**.

Types of radioactive decay

Decay happens because of something called the **weak nuclear force**. This is a force that mainly affects protons and neutrons. It makes unstable atoms lose energy – stabilizing them – in various different ways. Here are two of them.

Beta minus decay
(ß- decay)

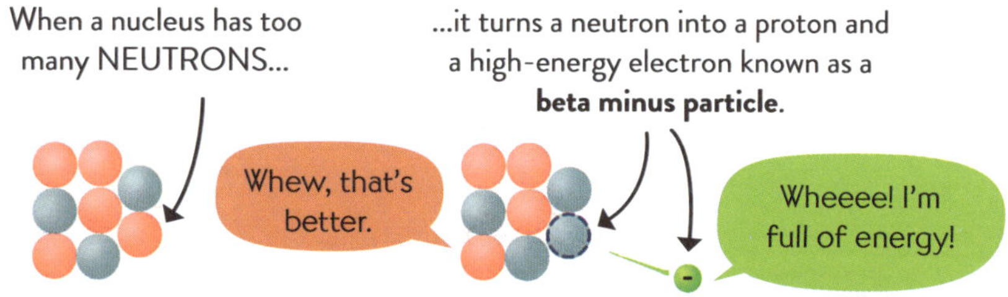
When a nucleus has too many NEUTRONS...
Whew, that's better.
...it turns a neutron into a proton and a high-energy electron known as a **beta minus particle**.
Wheeee! I'm full of energy!

Beta plus decay
(ß+ decay)

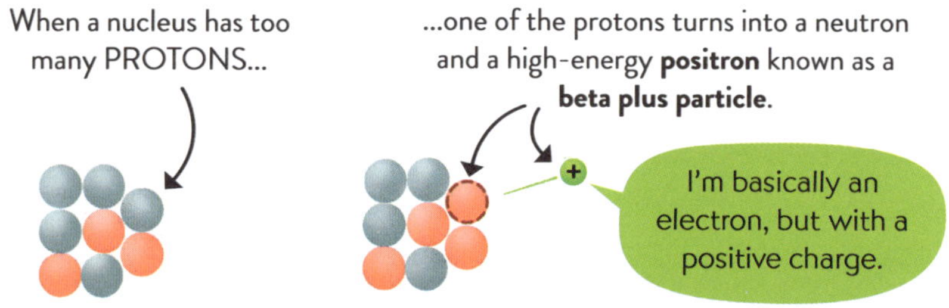
When a nucleus has too many PROTONS...
...one of the protons turns into a neutron and a high-energy **positron** known as a **beta plus particle**.
I'm basically an electron, but with a positive charge.

Beta particles are examples of something called **radiation**, and they can be dangerous. Both kinds of beta decay also produce particles called **neutrinos** – a kind of radiation that is harmless.

A dangerous discovery

The term **radioactivity** was first used by physicist Marie Curie. She realized that radiation was caused by something *inside* atoms. She became the first person to win two Nobel prizes, and greatly advanced our knowledge of nuclear physics, but her work with radioactivity eventually caused her death.

I worked with radioactive metals all my life. What I didn't know was that they were constantly bombarding my body with invisible particles.
Those particles can damage cells in the body. Because I was exposed to so much radiation for so long, in the end it gave me a fatal blood disease.

You can't tell by looking that these lumps of metal are dangerous.

Is radiation helpful or dangerous?

Although exposure to radiation *can* be deadly, radioactivity is also a perfectly natural (and very important) process – and it can be harnessed for good.

Radiation makes life possible – it's what makes the Sun shine. Radioactive particles without enough energy to damage our bodies are all around us all the time.

However radioactive particles with a *lot* of energy can cause huge amounts of death and destruction. It's impossible to say if radiation is good or bad.

Ways that radioactivity is helpful...

X-rays are a type of radiation that hospitals can use to find broken bones.

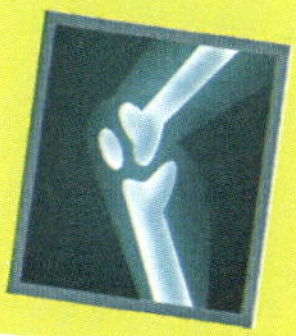

Doctors can use small amounts of a radioactive substance, which can be tracked around the body to find blockages or damage to blood vessels.

Sources of radiation often last a long time. They are used as fuel – especially by satellites or probes in space, where replacing batteries is impossible.

Radioactive atoms decay at a steady rate. This means scientists can estimate how many atoms in an object have already decayed. This allows them to work out how old the object is – even if it's *millions* of years old.

Nuclear power uses radiation to produce energy that doesn't add to global warming.

Ways that radioactivity is dangerous...

Exposure to lots of radiation at once, or small amounts over a long time, can lead to fatal radiation sickness or cancer.

Radioactive materials can release deadly radiation for millions of years, and can travel through most materials unless they're very dense. This makes storing them safely difficult and expensive.

Radioactive chemicals can be used to make nuclear weapons – possibly the most devastating weapons ever created.

If a nuclear power plant melts down, the radiation released can make the area deadly for millions of years.

The smallest things of all

Physicists try to identify the very smallest things – or "building blocks" – that make up the universe. And it turns out that *even* protons and neutrons are made up of *SMALLER* particles...

Peering into protons

Physicists have been discussing the idea of smaller and smaller particles since the nucleus was first discovered in 1911. It wasn't until the 1970s that the first **colliders** – or **particle accelerators** – were built. These machines enabled physicists to break open protons and neutrons to discover what was inside.

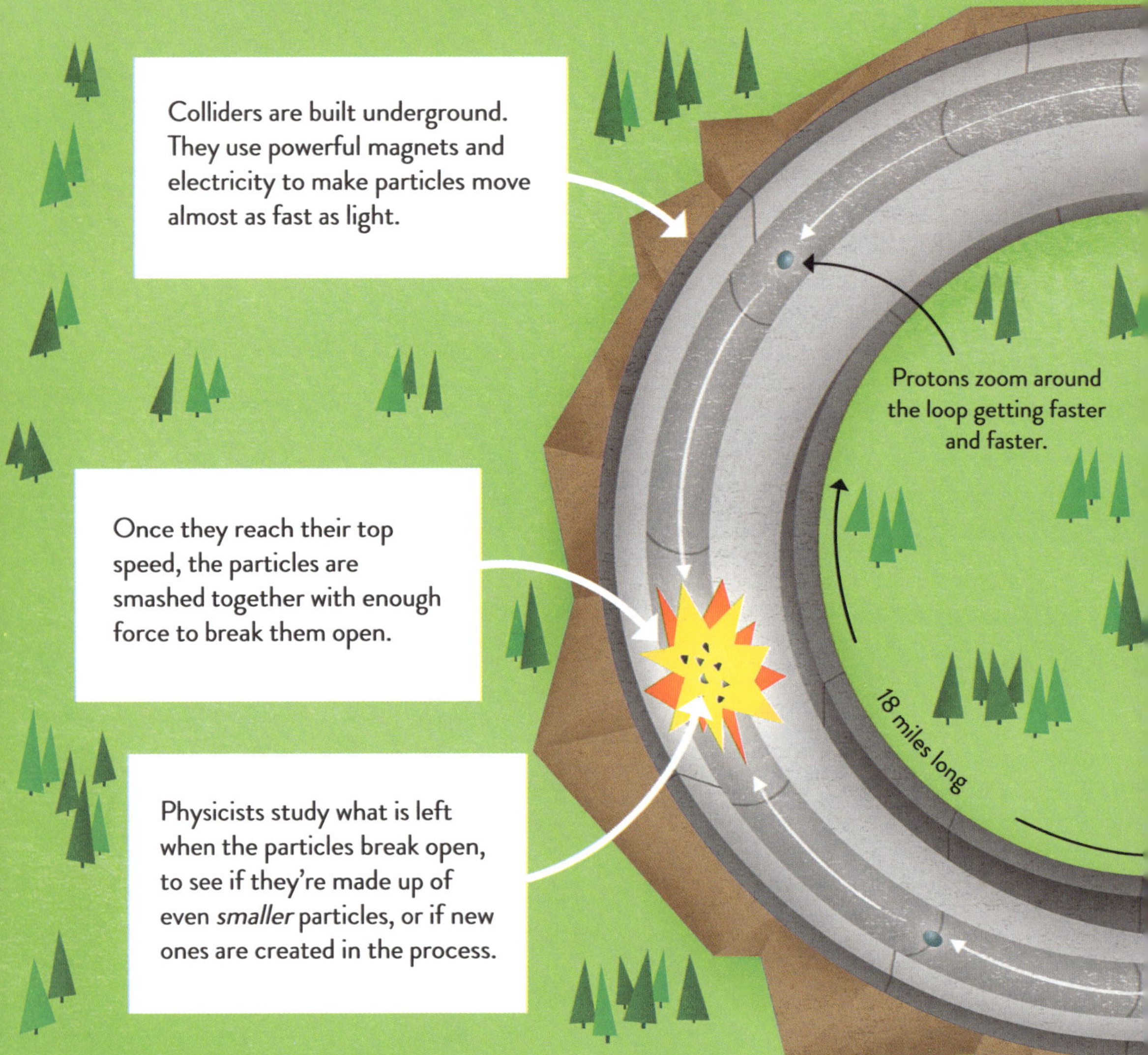
Colliders are built underground. They use powerful magnets and electricity to make particles move almost as fast as light.
Protons zoom around the loop getting faster and faster.
Once they reach their top speed, the particles are smashed together with enough force to break them open.
18 miles long
Physicists study what is left when the particles break open, to see if they're made up of even *smaller* particles, or if new ones are created in the process.

What scientists have discovered from these colliders is that protons and neutrons are only the beginning...

The Particle Zoo

Colliders soon revealed *lots* of new particles. Eventually physicists developed a system of classifying them, known as the **Standard Model**. The particles discovered don't *seem* to be made of anything smaller – so physicists call them **fundamental particles**.

Up is my favorite!
NO! I like Charm best!!

Quarks

QUARKS are particles that can combine in different ways to make larger particles, such as protons and neutrons. There are six different types of quarks.

Up
Down
Strange
Charm
Bottom
Top

Leptons

LEPTONS don't experience the strong nuclear force, so can't be glued to other particles. There are six types of leptons, too.

Electron
Muon
Tau
Electron neutrino
Muon neutrino
Tau neutrino

Bosons

BOSONS allow forces to work. Five fundamental bosons have been discovered – but physicists think there *might* be another, which they call the **graviton**.

Photon
Gluon
W boson
Z boson
Higgs boson
Graviton

With stronger colliders, we might, one day, find something new inside these particles.
It's the job of scientists to keep testing our theories to see if they still work!

Setting the scale

It's hard to wrap your head around just how unbelievably small the scales we're talking about are. A single atom is about *half a nanometer* across. To try to picture that, imagine a single grain of sand. Just that one grain contains roughly *43 quintillion* atoms.

43 quintillion?
That's 43,000,000,000,000,000,000.
Inside just one grain.

And remember that atoms are almost completely empty. The space between the positive nucleus and the clouds of negative electrons is most of the atom's size.

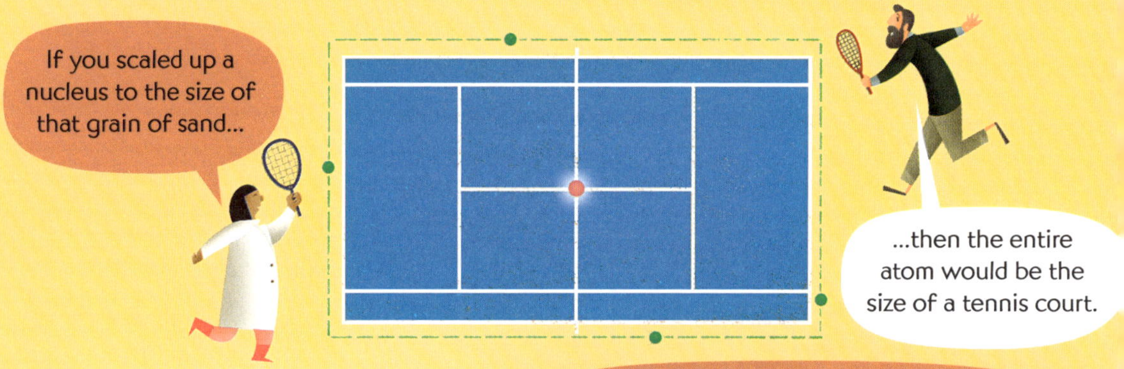

If you scaled up a nucleus to the size of that grain of sand...
...then the entire atom would be the size of a tennis court.

And if you scaled up just a single *proton* (or neutron) to be the size of a grain of sand...
...then the entire atom would be around the size of two soccer fields laid end to end.

Getting fundamental

The fundamental particles of the Standard Model are *100 million times smaller* than an individual atom.

If a *quark* was the size of a grain of sand, then the entire atom would be ten times bigger than London, UK.

Fundamental particles are so small, it's not possible to measure their size, or even see them under the most powerful microscopes. But they have other properties that physicists *can* measure.

Mass – how heavy the particle is

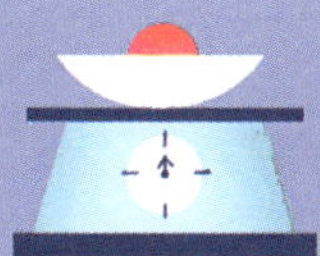

Speed – how fast the particle is going

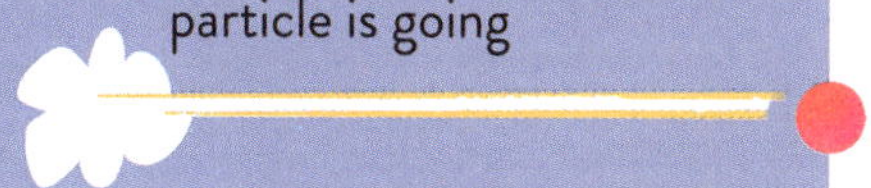

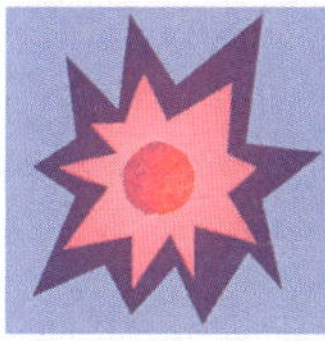

How much energy the particle has

Position – where in space the particle is

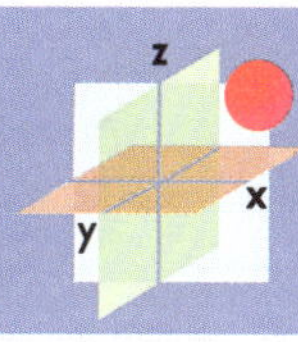
z
x
y

Spin – a property that affects how a particle moves through magnetic fields

Charge – how positive or negative the particle is

-
+

The weird thing is – measuring one of these properties can stop you from measuring another. This is one of the bizarre rules of **quantum mechanics**. Find out about *that* in the next chapter, starting on page 75.

Subatomic interactions

So what do all these particles actually *do*? The simple answer is that they **interact** with each other. It doesn't sound like much – but those interactions create all the matter, forces and energy in the universe.

Here's an example involving quarks and gluons. They interact to make protons and neutrons, and they're responsible for the strong nuclear force, too.

Individual protons and neutrons are made up of three **quarks**. These quarks are held in place because they pass particles known as **gluons** between them. A quark "catches" a gluon thrown out by another quark, and then "throws" it out to the next quark. This game of catch pulls the quarks together, holding them in place as either a proton or a neutron.

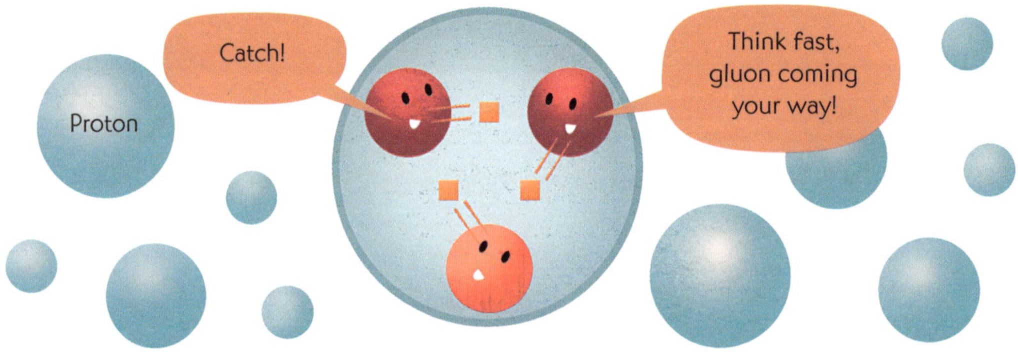

Catch!
Proton
Think fast, gluon coming your way!

Gluons only exist on their own in the tiny spaces inside protons and neutrons. Meanwhile, protons and neutrons pass bundles of quarks to each other, which glues these larger particles together to make a nucleus.

Playing quark catch really brings us together.
Neutron

These interactions happen constantly in all atoms at almost the speed of light. The force of these interactions is what binds the nucleus together so tightly, and it's why scientists call this interaction the *strong* nuclear force. It's not really possible to explain *why* this happens, it just *does*.

The secret behind electromagnetism

Some quarks and leptons have an electric charge, which comes about because they pass things known as **virtual particles** to each other. These are like normal particles, that only exist for a small amount of time. But they're the secret behind electromagnetism.

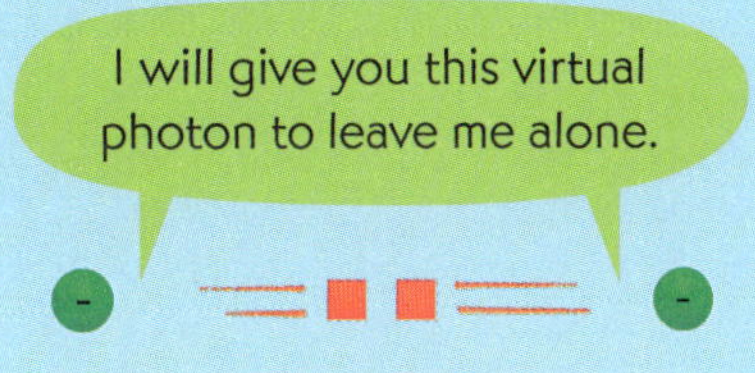
I will give you this virtual photon to leave me alone.

If both particles, such as two electrons, have the same charge, they pass **virtual photons** to each other constantly. This is what pushes them apart.

Take this virtual photon as a token of our friendship.

When two particles have opposite charges, say, a proton and an electron, only one gives a virtual photon to the other. This pulls them together.

Exchanging virtual photons is what keeps electrons orbiting an atom's nucleus. It's also what allows atoms to join together to make stuff – such as this book, and YOU.

Making bosons

When protons and neutrons change during radioactive decay, the energy they lose is thrown out as a particle called a **W boson**. This happens because of a force – the one physicists call the **weak nuclear force**.

Protons are made from two up quarks, and one down quark.

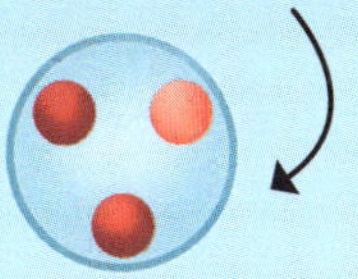

If a nucleus has too *many* protons, then it's unstable.

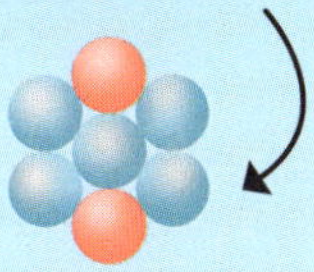

One of the quarks changes from up to down. By doing so, it loses energy in the form of a W boson.

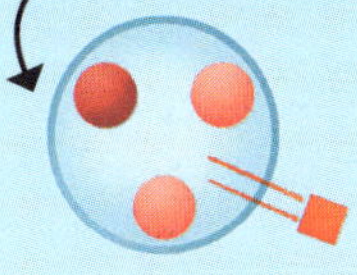

The proton becomes a neutron, making the nucleus stable. The W boson becomes a **beta particle** (see page 62).

These are just some of the main ways particles interact to create the world as we know it.

Wait – what about gravity, does *that* have a particle?
Well, there might be such a thing as a graviton, but we haven't seen it – YET.

It's only a theory

The Standard Model of particles is considered one of *the* most successful scientific theories *ever*. So far, all of its predictions of a new particle, or interaction between particles, have gone on to be found in nature. Here's an example of a success story, to do with **mass**.

If photons are essentially the same size as quarks, why do they have less mass?
Where does mass even come from?
Maybe all the particles are acted on by *something* – some particles more than others?
Something in the Standard Model we've never seen before!

Moving through fields

Sometimes, the answer to a physics puzzle requires an idea that's hard to picture. All forces work by using one of the fundamental particles, and physicists describe those particles as moving through **fields.** These fields are unique to each of the forces. You can picture it like this...

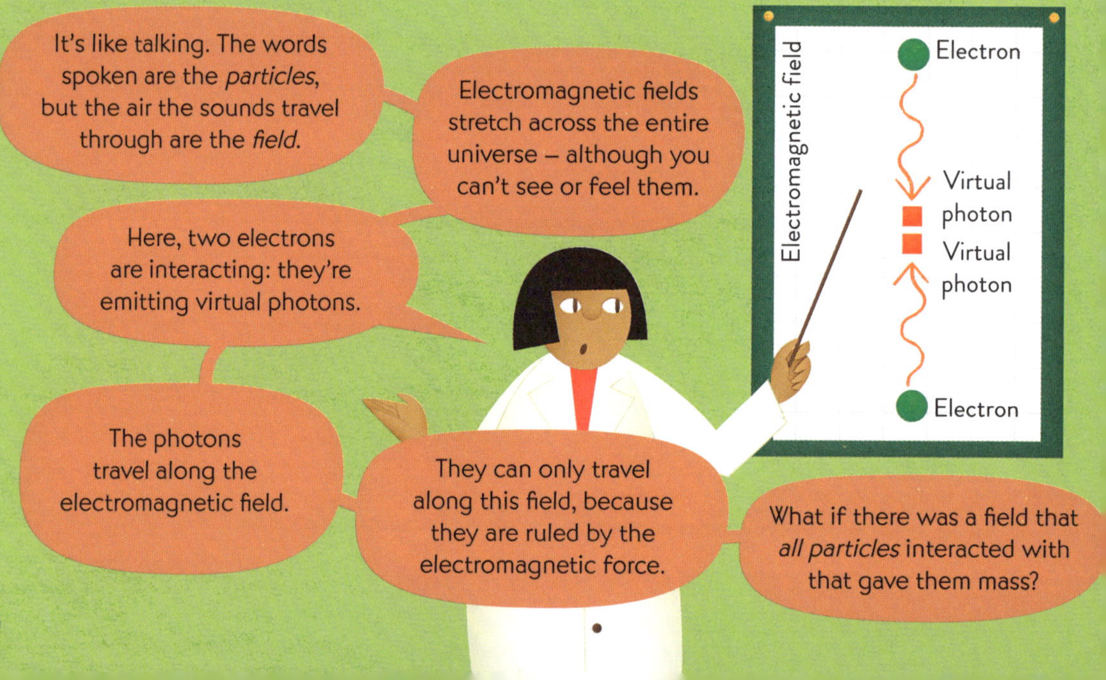

It's like talking. The words spoken are the *particles*, but the air the sounds travel through are the *field*.
Electromagnetic fields stretch across the entire universe – although you can't see or feel them.
Here, two electrons are interacting: they're emitting virtual photons.
The photons travel along the electromagnetic field.
They can only travel along this field, because they are ruled by the electromagnetic force.
What if there was a field that *all particles* interacted with that gave them mass?
Electromagnetic field
Electron
Virtual photon
Virtual photon
Electron

The Higgs boson

In 1964, physicists suggested that there *was* a field that all particles interacted with, and it's how much they interact with this field that gives particles different masses. It was named the **Higgs field**, after one of the physicists who predicted it.

Think of the Higgs field as a field of snow that you're rolling balls over.
Sounds weird, but just trust me.
Higgs
SPLAT
ZIPPP
A bowling ball sinks, and so can't roll very quickly. It interacts with the field strongly, which is why it has a large mass.
On the other hand, a ping-pong ball barely interacts at all. It can zoom along the surface very quickly. It has a small mass.

The idea of the Higgs field explained the mystery of the Standard Model's differing masses. But fields are invisible and undetectable, so to prove it physicists needed evidence of a particle that makes the field work. The **Higgs boson**.

1
Grrrr
BASH
Producing Higgs bosons will mean smashing particles together with more energy than ever before.

2
In September 2008, scientists in Switzerland turned on the Large Hadron Collider – the most powerful particle accelerator ever built – to do just that.

3
The machine produced huge amounts of data to examine. It wasn't until July 2012 that scientists were confident that they'd seen evidence of the Higgs boson.

4 Finding that boson gave even more support to the Standard Model theory, making it a champion among scientific theories.

But it could still turn out to be wrong. Or, at least, it might not be the whole story.

Back to the big things

All the particles in this chapter are combined in a lot of ways, to create EVERYTHING around us. One of the biggest things they make are stars. In fact, stars are so huge that they squash the atoms inside them – fusing them together. This process is known as **NUCLEAR FUSION**.

All stars are filled with hydrogen atoms – each of which contain one proton.

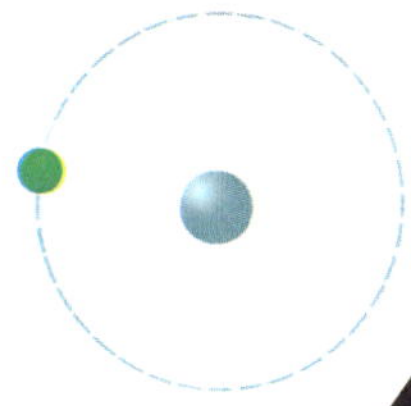

The *extreme* temperatures inside a star give these protons lots of energy, making them move at massive speeds.

Hot, hot, hot!!
Hey! I'm zoomin' here!
Wheeeee!

The core of a star is under a huge amount of pressure, too – it holds vast numbers of protons in a small space.

I'm going too fast!
Brace for impact!
KABLAM!!

With not much space, and a lot of energy, protons start colliding together. This creates enough power for the strong nuclear force to fuse them together into bigger atoms.

Once the protons have fused, the weak nuclear force turns some of them into neutrons to create a stable nucleus.

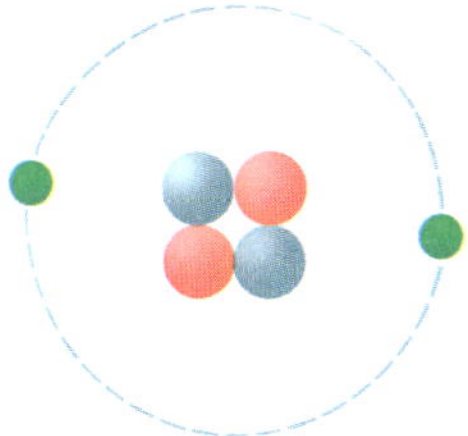

Then the star creates brand new atoms by fusing smaller atoms together.

The fusion process also releases a *lot* of energy – especially as heat and light. It's this process that makes stars shine.

So all stars are constantly smashing hydrogen atoms together in nuclear explosions? Wow!
That's right – even our own Sun! Fusion produces around four times more energy than fission, and much less toxic waste.
Why aren't we doing it on Earth then?
Well, we are trying to...

The temperature and pressure needed for fusion happens naturally inside stars. But they're very hard to achieve elsewhere.

This is a fusion reactor.

Fusion *has* been done here on Earth. But it took more energy to fuse just a few atoms than the process produced. Physicists are working on ways to make it more efficient and cost-effective.

Can a particle be
in two places at
the same time?

What's light
made from?

What does a quantum
computer do?

Are there
parallel universes?

Chapter 5
QUANTUM MECHANICS

If there's one thing physicists have discovered in the last hundred years, it's that the universe is even weirder than any earlier scientists expected.

Einstein's theories of relativity showed that reality didn't have to match our daily experiences. Time and space could be experienced at different rates by different objects. But then, a new theory arrived that took everything a step *farther*. This theory showed things being in two places at once, and behaving in two different ways at the same time.

This is called **QUANTUM MECHANICS**.

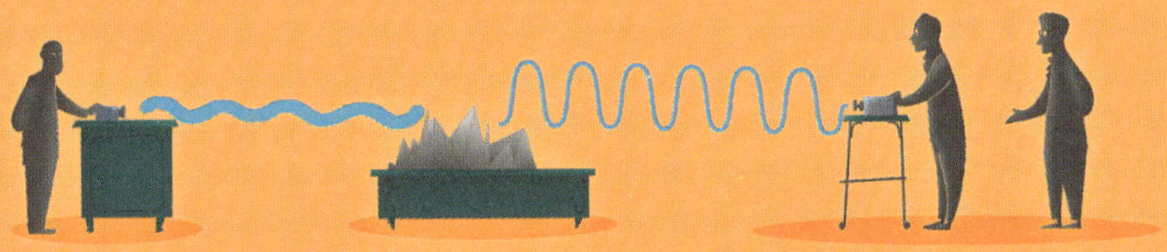

What IS quantum mechanics?

Oooh, I've heard of that. It's supposed to be incredibly exciting, but *super* complicated.
It IS incredibly exciting. But it's not so complicated. There are a couple of things to explain first, though...

First, quantum mechanics is all about the very tiniest particles, such as electrons and photons. They're things we can *feel the effects of*, but not things we can actually *observe*.

Here are some small things you CAN see – even if you need a powerful microscope.

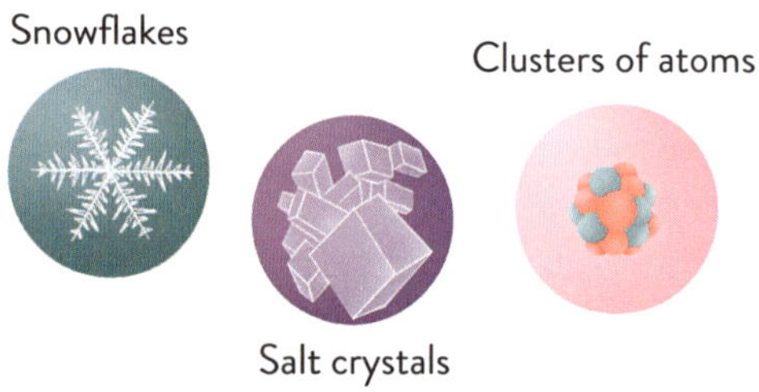
Snowflakes
Clusters of atoms
Salt crystals

It's hard to draw pictures of things that exist at the quantum scale – subatomic particles and such.

Here are some small things you CAN'T see, no matter what equipment you use.

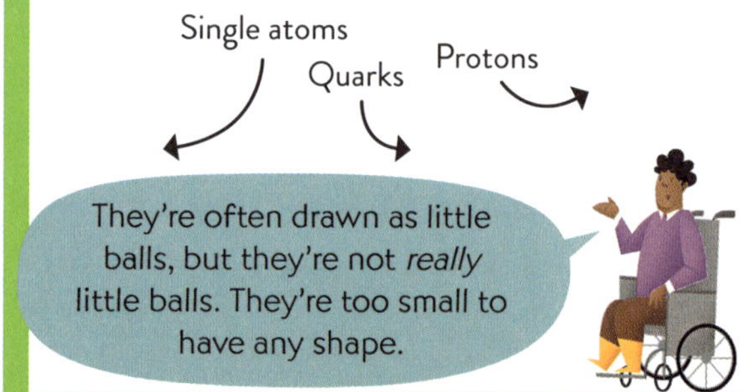
Single atoms
Quarks
Protons
They're often drawn as little balls, but they're not *really* little balls. They're too small to have any shape.

Compared to atoms, we live in a world of BIG things. Our brains have learned how to make sense of how big things work. That could mean anything from grains of sand to trees, and even whole planets.

Even though we're made of tiny particles, we have no way to watch them working. This means the way they actually behave doesn't make "sense" in the way that, say, gravity does.

If you push a tree hard enough...
...it'll fall down.
That's gravity at work.

What happens if you push an electron?
Sorry, that *question itself* doesn't make sense. It's just not possible to touch an electron, let alone *push* one.

So *how* do physicists make sense of quantum mechanics?
Math. LOTS of math.
No problem! I'm great at math.
Math is so cool. Our brains can make sense of numbers and symbols, even when they're describing things that we can't see, or draw pictures of, or really even think about.
Give me an example.
$H(t)|\psi(t)\rangle = i\hbar\frac{\partial}{\partial t}|\psi(t)\rangle$
Oh golly...
Oh it's not so bad. You just have to learn what each symbol stands for.
The main thing about the math used in quantum mechanics is that it doesn't lead to *specific* answers. Instead, it's about predicting a range of the MOST LIKELY answers.
You mean, it's about **probability**?
Yes, exactly. When it comes to subatomic particles, you can never know EXACTLY what a *single particle* is up to. But you CAN – with a kind of math called probability – predict what a *large number of particles* are *likely to be doing.*

Quantum basics

The term **quantum** means a "packet of energy." It was invented by physicists who were trying to find out what energy actually *is*...

Electrons and light

Here's a physics fact: when light is shone on objects, especially metal objects, they emit electrons. Physicists call this the **PHOTOELECTRIC EFFECT**. But the *rules* behind this phenomenon were confusing to the physicists who were studying it 100 years ago...

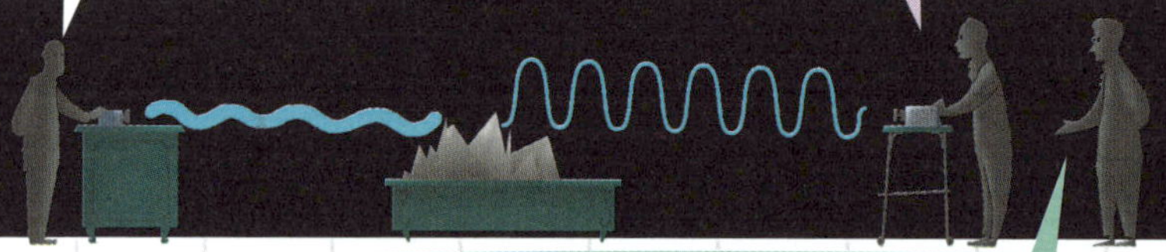
Let's try shining a *brighter* light. That should mean the electrons that are emited have *more* energy.
Now let's try increasing the *frequency* of the light waves we're using. That means waves of light will hit more often, so the metal should emit *more* electrons.
Hang on, what we see happening is the *exact opposite*?! Brighter light gives us *more electrons*, while higher frequency light gives us *more energetic* electrons.

In the 1920s, some argued that the photoelectric effect made sense if you thought of light as tiny packets of energy, or particles. They named them **photons**.

The brighter the light, the more photons the light is made of. The energy of the photons doesn't increase – there are just more of them.

The frequency of a particle is how fast it's vibrating, and that is how much energy it has. So high frequency photons pass on MORE energy to the electrons in the metal.

It was Albert Einstein who first suggested the existence of photons some years earlier. It seemed to him to solve the mystery of the photoelectric effect...

But wait, I thought light was a wave?

Particles or waves?

The discovery of photons was a surprise. Most physicists understood that light was a kind of WAVE – with wavelength, frequency and all the other properties of a wave. So, many were puzzled as to how a *particle* could move like a *wave*.

Moving in waves

Here's an experiment physicists used to demonstrate light behaving as a wave.

They shone a beam of light through a screen...
...that had two slits in it...
...and measured the light using a light detector placed behind the screen.

What happened was, waves of light split into two after passing through the slits, and this created a distinctive pattern on the detector.

Light moves as a single wave, until the two slits in the screen split the wave into two.
The two waves overlap, meaning they hit the detector in a particular way.
They hit a detector, and create a series of dark and light patches. This is called an **interference pattern**.
Light source
Light waves
Light detector
Scratch
OK, so light IS made of waves, then. Simple.
But light is made of particles! Einstein said so.
It's more complicated than that I'm afraid. Turn the page to find out more...

Electrons getting excited

Some atoms give off photons when they get heated up. This is because they start vibrating, which makes the electrons *in them* get *excited*. Excited electrons start to move – and give off photons. This happens in a particular way.

I'm an electron, and I'm orbiting my atom's nucleus. I have to stay on this orbit zone – I can't just go a little closer or a little farther. Unless...

...I get *excited*. Then I can jump up to a higher orbit zone. Up here, I'm vibrating faster than I was before – I have more energy.

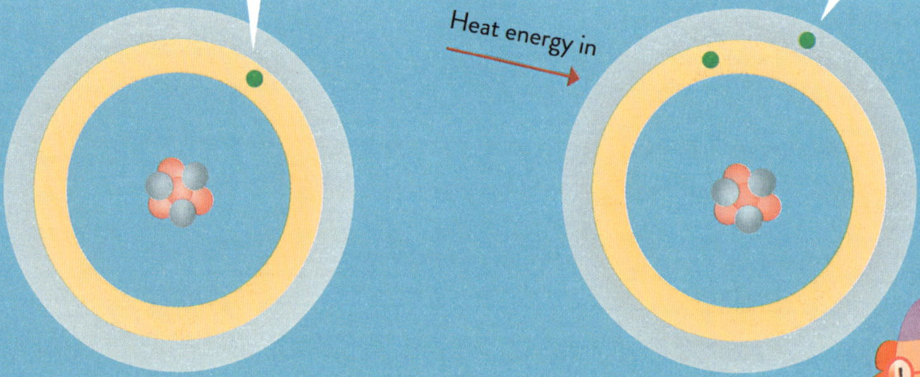

Electrons can get *less* excited, too. Here's what happens.

If I get less excited, I have to drop down to the lower orbit zone again. I lose some of my energy – and that energy becomes *light*.

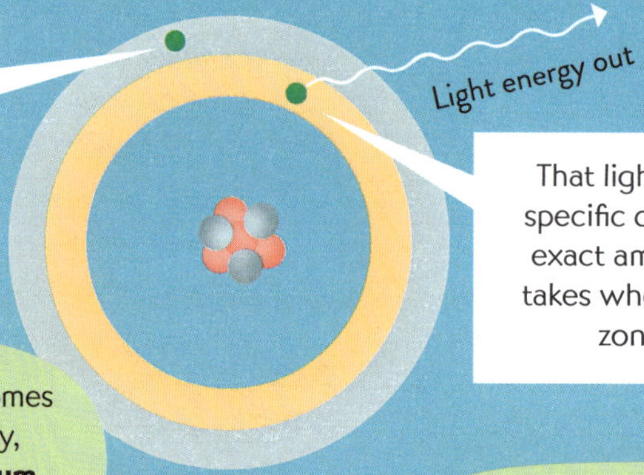

That light can only have a specific color, matching the exact amount of energy it takes when I drop from one zone to another.

Light emitted by electrons comes in a single packet of energy, which scientists call a **quantum**. this is where *quantum mechanics* gets its name.

In this example, each "quantum of light" is a photon.

So why does light *behave* like a wave if we know that it's *made of* particles? That's where the world of quantum mechanics starts to get *really* weird.

Particles *and* waves

Photons explain the photoelectric effect, and the colors of light given off by excited electrons. But the double-slit experiment can only be explained if light is a wave. So which is it? The answer is that light is *both*.

Even if you do the double-slit experiment with a photon emitter, a device that only ejects one photon at a time, you *still* get an interference pattern. This is only possible with a wave.
A single particle such as photon can't be interfering with anything other than itself...
...unless it's going through both slits at once...?
So physicists tried to catch the photons in the act of passing through two slits at the same time.
Wait, now the photons are only going through *one* slit and the interference pattern has vanished!
Instead we get two small sets of dots on the detector. This shows the photons are behaving like particles.

If nobody observes which path each photon chooses, then the photons take *both paths simultaneously* and spread out on the detector in the same way as a wave. Amazingly, if someone watches, then the photons act like individual particles. The only explanation is that they're waves and particles *at the same time*.

It's as if the photons are shy. When we *observe* them going through, they hide their ability to be in two places at once.
But when we're *not* observing, they behave like a wave and *do* go through both slits at once.
Nothing special to see here...
Quick, do the two-places-at-once trick!

Physicists call this **wave-particle duality**. It means *particles* sometimes have the properties of *waves*. It's not just photons that do this. The double-slit experiment has shown the same result with electrons, and even entire *atoms*.

Particles aren't shy, they're *uncertain*

The physicists who discovered wave-particle duality described these particles as "shy." But they discovered the problem wasn't with the particles – it was with the people trying to measure them. It turns out it's impossible to know more than one thing about what any single particle is up to.

Pick one: speed or location

It IS possible to know *where* a particle is, or *how fast* it's moving. But it's NOT possible to know both things at once. This phenomenon is known as **Heisenberg's Uncertainty Principle**. People have tried to find a way around it, but they can't.

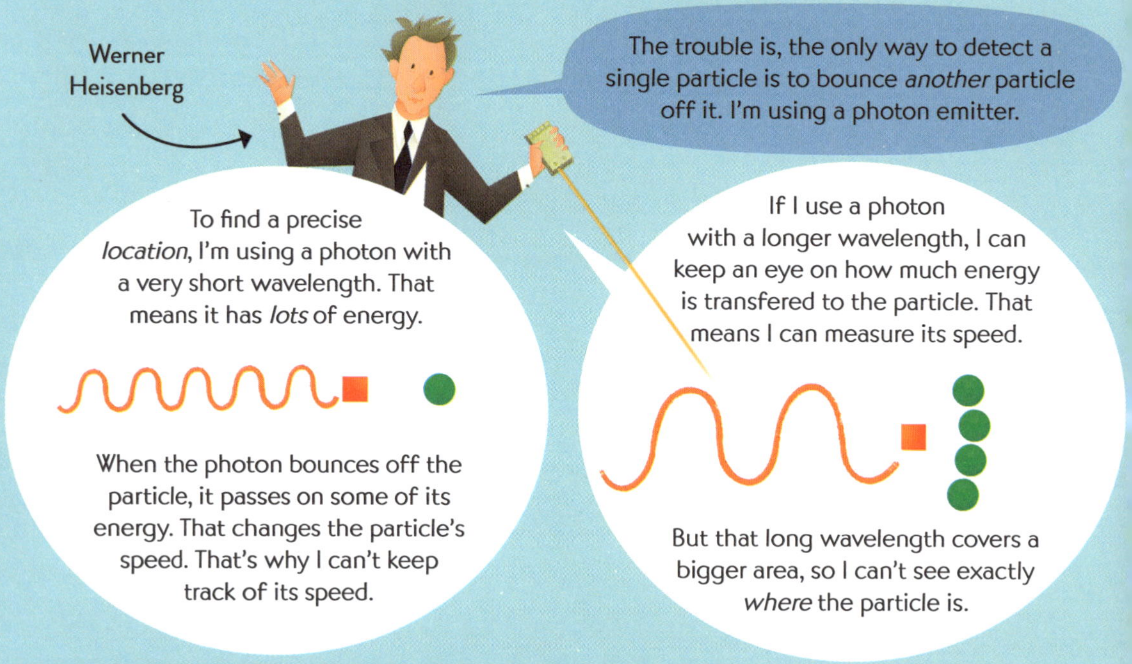
Werner Heisenberg
The trouble is, the only way to detect a single particle is to bounce *another* particle off it. I'm using a photon emitter.
To find a precise *location*, I'm using a photon with a very short wavelength. That means it has *lots* of energy.
When the photon bounces off the particle, it passes on some of its energy. That changes the particle's speed. That's why I can't keep track of its speed.
If I use a photon with a longer wavelength, I can keep an eye on how much energy is transfered to the particle. That means I can measure its speed.
But that long wavelength covers a bigger area, so I can't see exactly *where* the particle is.

In fact, we can never pinpoint EXACTLY the location or speed of a particle, in part because the *act of observing* a particle changes those things. All physicists can do is say roughly what area a particle is in, and roughly how fast it's moving.

For example, we might know there's an electron in an atom, and we know it's not in the nucleus – but we don't know *where* exactly it is.
But we can use math to predict where that electron is going to be, and how fast it'll be moving. For such tiny particles, a prediction is enough to work with.

What you CAN know: wavefunctions

Uncertainty might sound frustrating, but quantum physicists don't mind. That's because they *can* be certain about something called a particle's **wavefunction**. That means "the combination of all possible states a particle can be found in."

But what does *that* mean? Well, imagine that's there a room with a roast chicken on a table. There's also a hungry dog in the room. And a vacuum cleaner, a ball and a paint set. You can't see into the room, but you CAN build up a wavefunction of all possible things that might be happening in the room. And you can guess how *likely* each of those things is.

The dog is eating the chicken: VERY LIKELY
The dog is sleeping: QUITE LIKELY
The dog is chewing the ball: QUITE LIKELY
The dog is vacuuming: NOT VERY LIKELY
The dog is painting: NOT VERY LIKELY
Z Z Z

Using words, it's not possible to list every possible thing that might be in this wavefunction. But using math, you CAN. The main thing is, until you open the door, you don't KNOW what is happening. But you do know that *something* must be happening. A quantum physicist describes this total set of possibilities as "the dog being in a **superposition** on the wavefunction."

When we open the door and observe the dog, the wavefunction **collapses**.
Now that we know exactly what the dog is doing, the chance of it doing any of the other things is zero.
What's that got to do with photons, electrons and all that?
The dog is like one of those particles. The wavefunction of the particles means "all the places that particle could be." And to make predictions about what the particle is doing, you only need to know the wavefunction.
Wuff!

A quantum universe

Once physicists started to understand the way *tiny* particles behaved, they began to wonder what it might all mean for the world of BIG things – including YOU. After all, *everything* is made of these uncertain, unpredictable particles...

Hang on a minute – do *I* have a wavefunction?
Yes! Everything does, in fact. However, the more particles something contains, the smaller its wavefunction becomes.
What does that mean?
It means that the chances of any really unusual things happening to you are VERY small.
But they could still happen?
Well, according to quantum theory, part of your wavefunction says that every part of your body might decide to go through two different doors at once...
...but it's so, SO unlikely to happen that there's no point worrying about it.
Look, I'm still a little lost about how a wavefunction works. What's ACTUALLY happening before a wavefunction collapses? Is it really true that every possibility is happening at the same time?
Congratulations! You've just walked through a door to one of the most heated arguments in all of physics...

How to interpret quantum mechanics

Physicists are confident that the concepts of wavefunctions, superpositions and collapsing are all true. Or, at least, they provide a *model* of how the world of tiny particles works that *appears* to be true. But there are at least two different ways to interpret what this means for the world of big things.

I follow the *Copenhagen Interpretation*. This says that a particle literally does exist in every possible state at once – until it's observed.
So, inside that closed room with the dog and the chicken, every possible thing that could be happening inside, IS HAPPENING.
How?? That's insane.
Well, here's the tricky part. As soon as you open the door, the wavefunction collapses, and only one thing *is* happening.
I bet it's that the dog is eating the chicken.
Yes, me too. And at this point, that one thing is also ALL THAT EVER *WAS* HAPPENING. The past itself is part of the wavefunction that collapses.
I follow the *Many Worlds Interpretation*. This also says that a particle literally does exist in every possible state at once, until it's observed.
The difference between our interpretations is that I think each possible state *is in its own separate universe*.
So I believe that every possible version of the dog and the chicken exists in parallel universes.
When I open the door – which collapses the wavefunction – what happens is that I am now part of *just one* of all those universes.
What happens to all the other universes?
I've no idea. But it's possible that they're ALL still out there. And new universes appear *every time* there's an uncertainty.
So, somewhere, there's a parallel universe where I am going through two doors at once?
According to the math, yes. But it's very unlikely you'll ever go there.

Arguments about *interpretations* of quantum mechanics are fascinating (and there are more than two interpretations), but it doesn't seem to matter which is correct. Quantum mechanics is used to develop all sorts of practical, real world things. Turn the page to see some examples.

Using quantum mechanics

For many physicists, *why* quantum mechanics works the way it does isn't the important thing. What matters is studying what can be done with the seemingly magical properties of fundamental particles.

Now you see me, now you don't

The uncertain quantum nature of particles leads to a strange property known as **quantum tunneling**. But what's that?

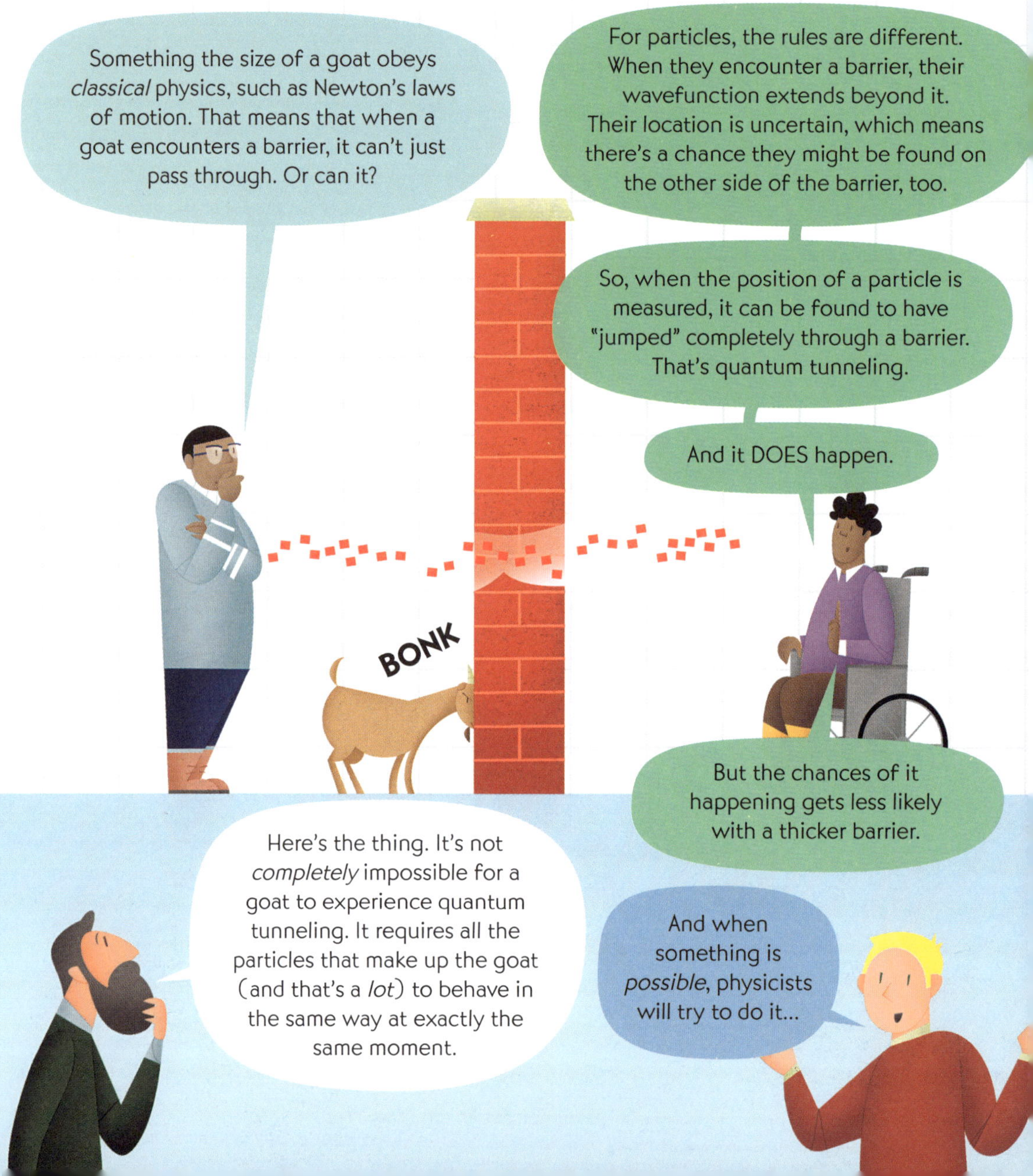
Something the size of a goat obeys *classical* physics, such as Newton's laws of motion. That means that when a goat encounters a barrier, it can't just pass through. Or can it?
For particles, the rules are different. When they encounter a barrier, their wavefunction extends beyond it. Their location is uncertain, which means there's a chance they might be found on the other side of the barrier, too.
So, when the position of a particle is measured, it can be found to have "jumped" completely through a barrier. That's quantum tunneling.
And it DOES happen.
BONK
But the chances of it happening gets less likely with a thicker barrier.
Here's the thing. It's not *completely* impossible for a goat to experience quantum tunneling. It requires all the particles that make up the goat (and that's a *lot*) to behave in the same way at exactly the same moment.
And when something is *possible*, physicists will try to do it...

Tunneling into the unknown

OK, so no one has managed to push a goat through a wall yet. But people have managed to harness the power of quantum tunneling, specifically to create amazingly powerful microscopes.

Normal microscopes have limits. If an object is smaller than the wavelength of visible light – say, a single atom – then it simply won't be visible under a normal microscope.
Light wave
Atom

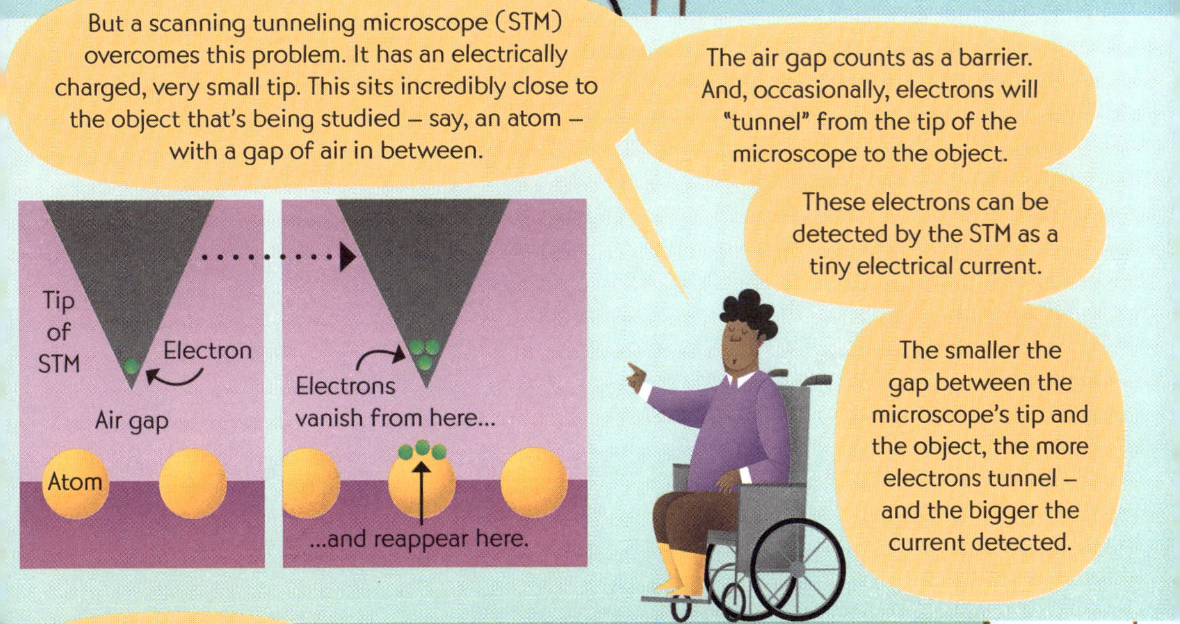

But a scanning tunneling microscope (STM) overcomes this problem. It has an electrically charged, very small tip. This sits incredibly close to the object that's being studied – say, an atom – with a gap of air in between.
Tip of STM
Electron
Air gap
Atom
Electrons vanish from here...
...and reappear here.
The air gap counts as a barrier. And, occasionally, electrons will "tunnel" from the tip of the microscope to the object.
These electrons can be detected by the STM as a tiny electrical current.
The smaller the gap between the microscope's tip and the object, the more electrons tunnel – and the bigger the current detected.

The STM uses computers to measure the movement of the tunneling electrons and build up a shape of the atoms in an object on a screen.
STMs can show atoms and how they combine to form matter. That's amazing! They're also used to help build up the parts that make computers work – parts that are only a few atoms big.

Tangled up

Another weird property of tiny particles is that they can affect one another even when separated by empty space. And this doesn't just apply over short distances, as with magnets, but can span *galaxies*. This is called **quantum entanglement**.

When physicists describe particles as being "entangled," what they mean is that the "state" of one particle instantly gives you information about the "state" of another. Imagine it like this...

You have a black marble and a white marble, each in a box that you can't see into.
The states of these two marbles are **entangled**. If you open one box and see a white marble, you know instantly that the other marble is black.
The marbles remain entangled, even if you separate the boxes by lightyears. Observing one marble tells you about the other, even if it's so far away you'll never *see* it.

It's possible for physicists to entangle a group of particles deliberately. This allows scientists to know about the state of some of the particles without ever observing them directly. It also means that, if they change the state of one particle, this changes the state of any particles it's entangled with.

Cool!
Cool? I think that's spooky.
It's cool AND a little spooky if you ask me. It also gives me an idea...

Beam me up, photon

Physicists realized that quantum entaglement might allow for something normally reserved for science fiction – **teleportation**. But, as with most things in quantum mechanics, the way this might work is... a little bit strange.

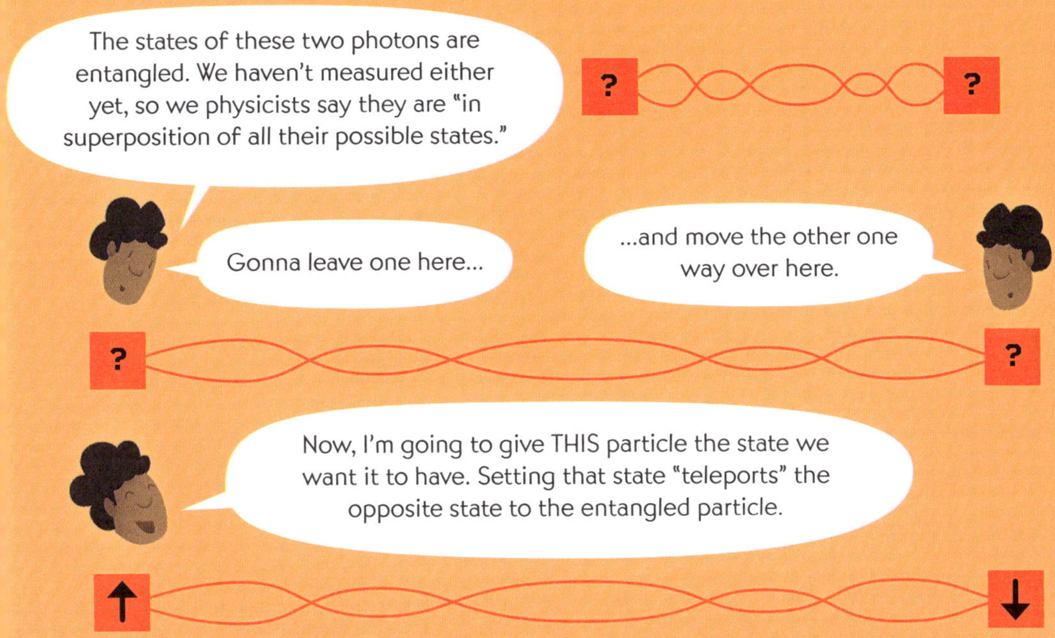
The states of these two photons are entangled. We haven't measured either yet, so we physicists say they are "in superposition of all their possible states."
?
?
Gonna leave one here...
...and move the other one way over here.
?
?
Now, I'm going to give THIS particle the state we want it to have. Setting that state "teleports" the opposite state to the entangled particle.

Teleportation sounds incredible – and it is. But physicists are a long way from beaming people across a *room*, let alone to other planets. Unfortunately, the larger an object, the smaller its wavefunction is, and the harder it is to entangle.

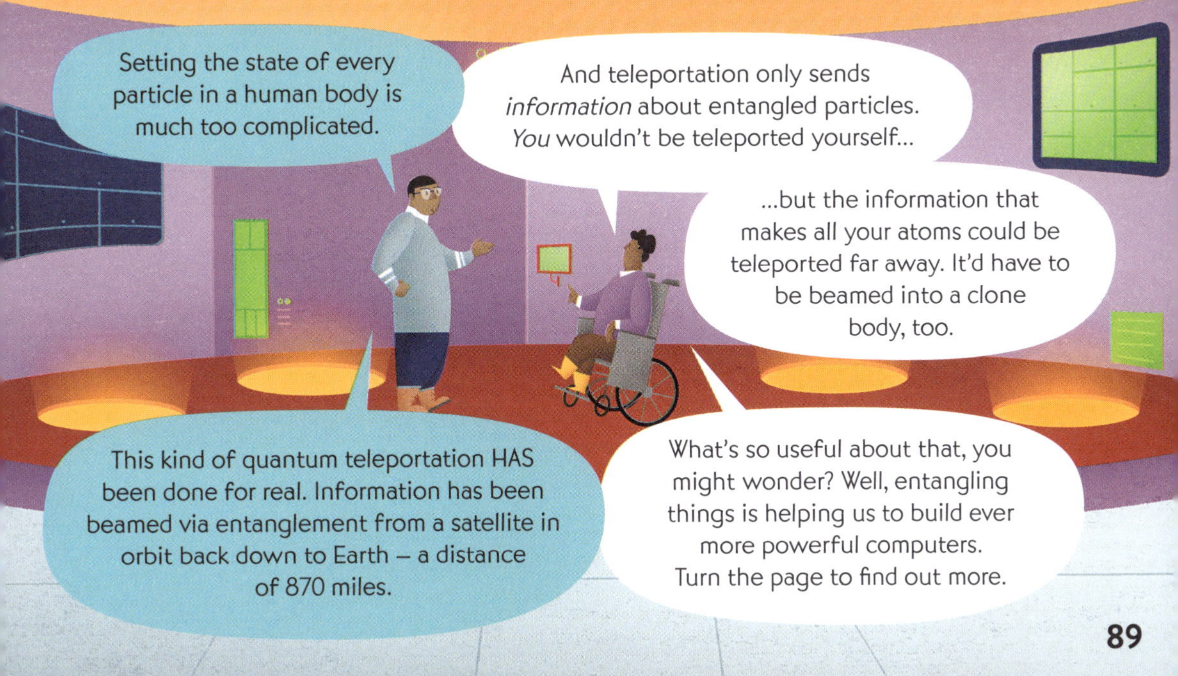
Setting the state of every particle in a human body is much too complicated.
And teleportation only sends *information* about entangled particles. *You* wouldn't be teleported yourself...
...but the information that makes all your atoms could be teleported far away. It'd have to be beamed into a clone body, too.
This kind of quantum teleportation HAS been done for real. Information has been beamed via entanglement from a satellite in orbit back down to Earth – a distance of 870 miles.
What's so useful about that, you might wonder? Well, entangling things is helping us to build ever more powerful computers. Turn the page to find out more.

Quantum computing

Computers store information using things called **bits.** A bit is basically a switch that can either be **on**, or **off**. This is enough to make a language that computers use to do all sorts of things, from solving sums to building the internet. Quantum computers will be able to use a more sophisticated language, enabling them to do more things, faster.

Quantum computers use **qubits** to store information. Qubits are quantum particles, and exist in a superposition of on and off *at the same time.*
...and that's useful, is it?
Very useful. Here, let's have a look at how a computer might solve a maze...

A normal computer needs to check every path one at a time, starting from the beginning again when it finds a dead end.

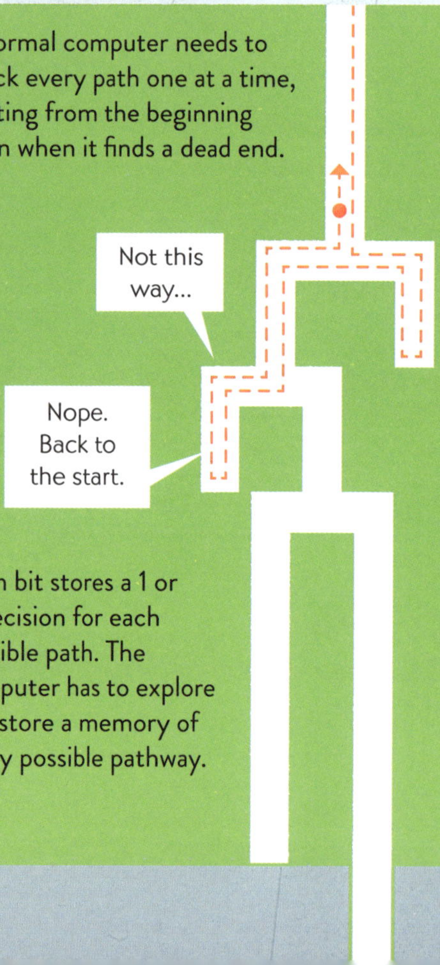
Not this way...
Nope. Back to the start.

Each bit stores a 1 or 0 decision for each possible path. The computer has to explore and store a memory of every possible pathway.

A quantum computer can try following two paths at the *same time.*

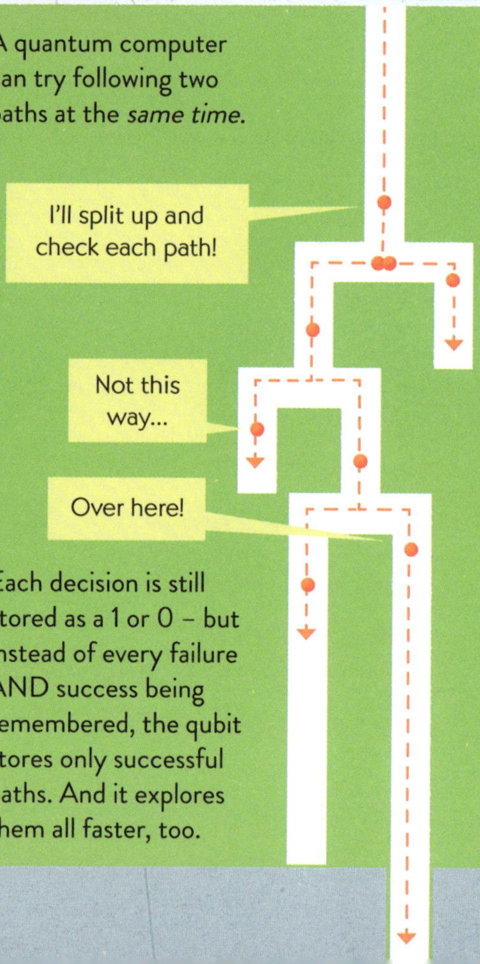
I'll split up and check each path!
Not this way...
Over here!

Each decision is still stored as a 1 or 0 – but instead of every failure AND success being remembered, the qubit stores only successful paths. And it explores them all faster, too.

The qubits in a quantum computer are *entangled* together. This means that different parts of a single computer can share information instantaneously, without needing to travel along circuits.

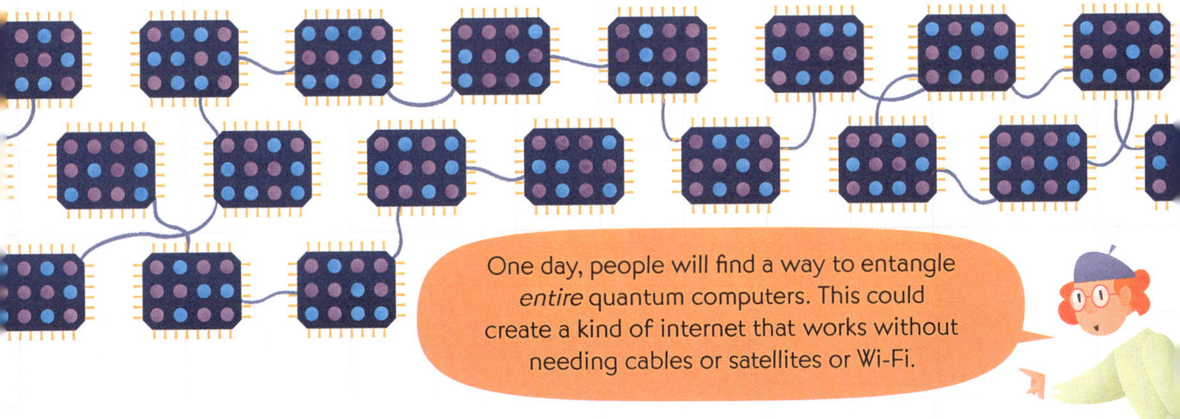
One day, people will find a way to entangle *entire* quantum computers. This could create a kind of internet that works without needing cables or satellites or Wi-Fi.

Quantum computers are much faster than normal computers. The ability of qubits to perform calculations simultaneously allows them to solve incredibly complex problems. Here are some of the possible uses of quantum computers.

They can crack codes quickly – and also help make passwords and information sharing more secure.

They can help predict weather patterns.

They can make models of medicines that would work better for individual people.

They may be able to create machines with artificial intelligence – machines that can think and even talk like people.

But it's VERY difficult to make qubits, and to link them together.

Qubits have to be in a superposition, which means they MUST be unobserved. As soon as they are observed, all their wavefunctions will collapse and the computing power will be lost.
The more qubits are added to a quantum computer, the harder it is to entangle their wavefunctions together.
But we're only a few years from completing a usable quantum computer!

How and when did the universe begin?

What happens if you fall into a black hole?

How do we know there are other galaxies out there?

What color are stars really?

Chapter 6
SPACE

The ultimate aim of physics is to produce very general theories that apply to *everything*. And the ultimate test of a theory is whether it can explain the whole of the universe. That means everything from large objects out in space, such as planets or black holes, to small things back home.

Astonishingly, physicists have been able to learn about what stars are made of, the origins of the universe and many, many other things – without even leaving our planet.

How the universe began

The biggest thing there is that anyone can investigate is, of course, the universe. But where do you even start? Well, at the beginning...
...and most physicists think it *began* with the **Big Bang**.

The Big Bang was *not* an explosion. It was a sudden, rapid EXPANDING of stuff. A little like a balloon being inflated very, very quickly.

How on earth did physicists arrive at such an idea? Well, it's to do with something they observed in the 1920s, called **REDSHIFT**.

Redshift

Distant objects in space give out light of different wavelengths, which can be seen as colors. But those wavelengths, and the colors, change depending on how an object is moving relative to us, either shifting towards blue, or towards red...

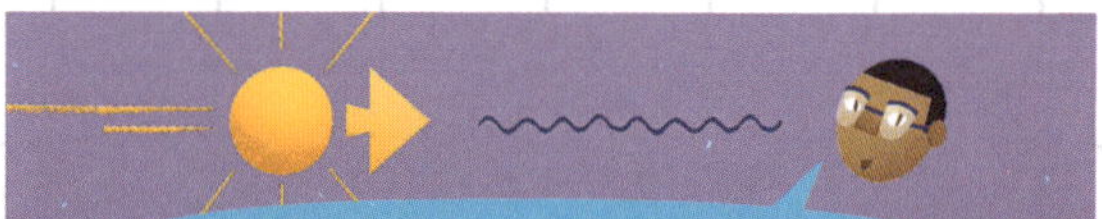

When an object moves quickly *towards* us, the light waves are squashed together, making the wavelength shorter. The object looks blue: this is **blueshift**.

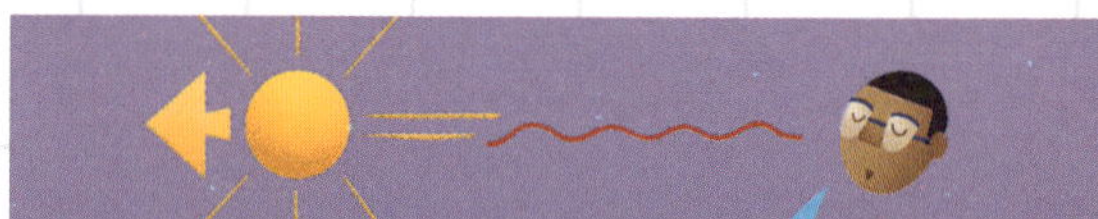

When it's moving quickly *away from* us, light waves are stretched apart and the wavelengths get longer. The object looks red: this is **redshift**.

~~BANG!~~
INFLATE

Time began roughly **13.8 billion years** ago.

The Big Bang and beyond

All there was, in the VERY beginning, was energy, and a very hot, dense point known as **INITIAL SINGULARITY.** No one knows what that was like. But physicists do know, in lots of detail, what happened next...

In a tiny fraction of the first second... the universe inflated from the size of an atom to the size of a grapefruit – and electrons and quarks formed.

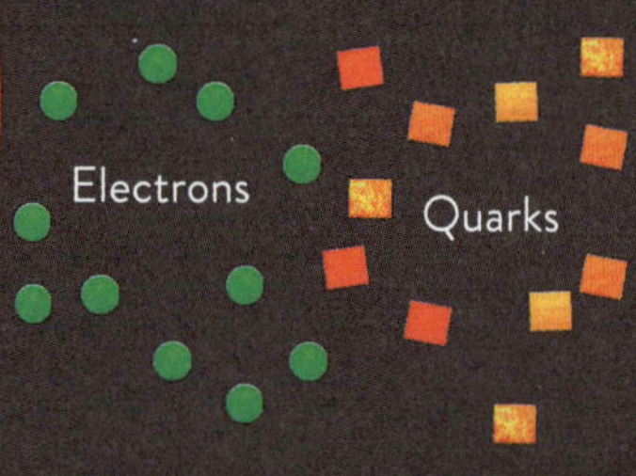

Less than a second later... quarks came together and formed the first protons and neutrons.

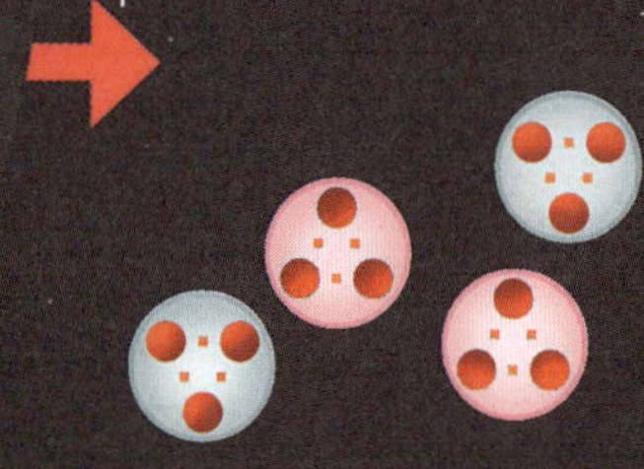

How we know about the Big Bang

It turns out that most large objects in space exhibit *redshift* – so they're moving *away from* us, and from each other. Physicists think this means things were once much closer together. They're moving apart because the universe started off by *expanding* – that's the Big Bang theory. Redshift suggests that the universe is *still* expanding, and showing no signs that it will ever stop. In fact, it's speeding up.

Physicists have also discovered something called **cosmic microwave background radiation**, or **CMBR** for short. This is the trace of extreme heat left over from the Big Bang that hasn't completely cooled down, even after billions of years.

Redshift, CMBR and many other observations have enabled physicists to piece together in detail what happened at the beginning of the universe.
Physicists have even been able to recreate the heat, pressure and density of the first second of the universe using a particle accelerator (like the one on page 64).

400,000 years later... electrons combined with protons and neutrons, forming the first atoms.

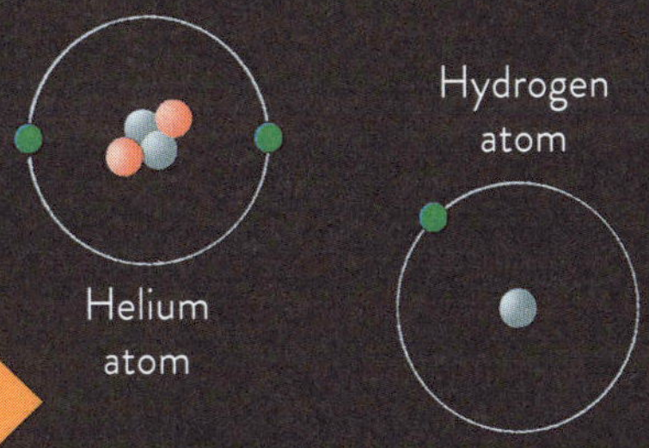
Helium atom
Hydrogen atom

Light began to shine.

Another 12.8 billion years later... a giant cloud of hydrogen and helium formed. Galaxies later formed from this.

Smaller clouds of gas collapsed to become the FIRST stars...

...which eventually exploded and formed NEW stars and planets.

Making sense of the sky

For thousands of years, people thought the Earth was at the center of the universe, and that all the other "heavenly bodies," as they called them – the Sun, the planets, the stars – revolved around it.

Modeling the solar system

Ancient thinkers came up with ingenious models to describe and predict how the heavenly bodies moved. Up to a point, the models worked quite well, but they were pretty complicated. This is what they thought.

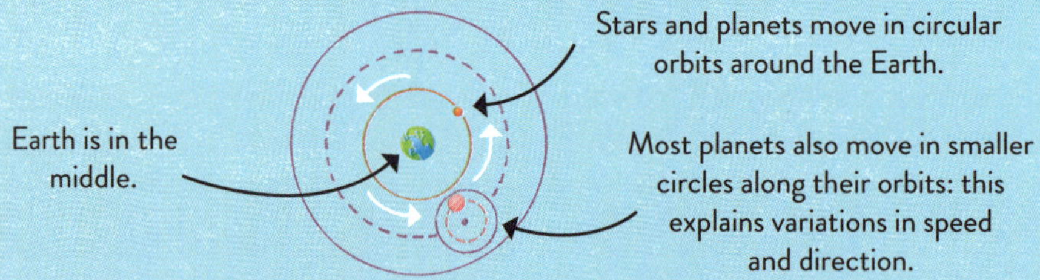
Stars and planets move in circular orbits around the Earth.
Earth is in the middle.
Most planets also move in smaller circles along their orbits: this explains variations in speed and direction.

As new observations were made, extra rotating segments had to be added to keep it all working. People even made physical versions of the models with moving parts. These were called armillary spheres or astrolabes.

Up-to-date models of the universe! Get 'em here!
For sale! Armillary spheres
You're going to have to add another ring, dude. Apollonius has just seen Mercury going backward!

Polish astronomer Nicolaus Copernicus began to wonder if the whole thing might work better if he put the Sun at the center of the universe.

Hmmm, I wonder if THIS makes more sense?

Copernicus's new model wasn't perfect, nor was it an instant success. Eventually, though, people began to accept the core idea and use it to develop new and more accurate models. There were, of course, always a few people who didn't agree...

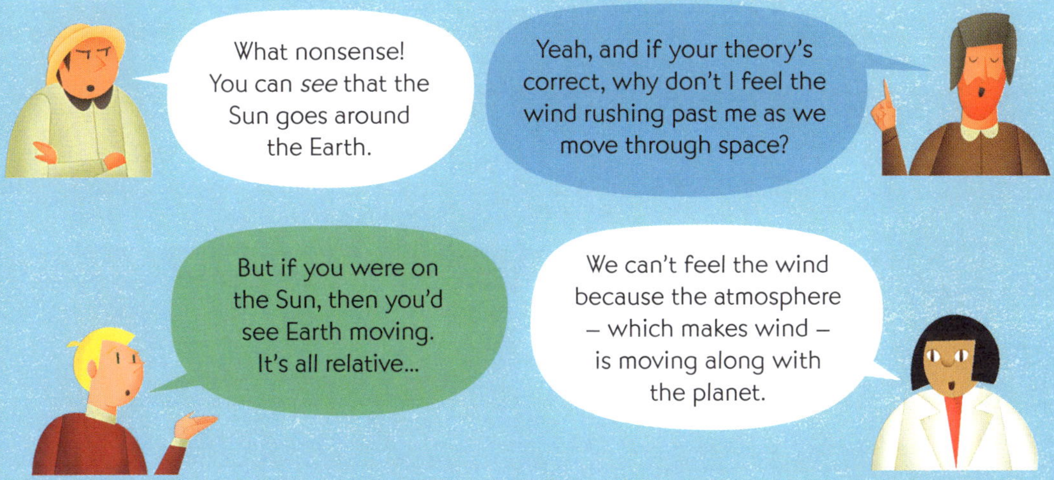
What nonsense! You can *see* that the Sun goes around the Earth.
Yeah, and if your theory's correct, why don't I feel the wind rushing past me as we move through space?
But if you were on the Sun, then you'd see Earth moving. It's all relative...
We can't feel the wind because the atmosphere – which makes wind – is moving along with the planet.

Going in circles (or not)

Whatever model people used, Mars was a problem planet. It sped up, it slowed down and sometimes it even went backward. The most up-to-date models couldn't predict its movements accurately.
It was 17th century astronomer Johannes Kepler who had a brainwave.

Mars' orbit is *oval-shaped*, not circular! Now if Mars does this, what about the other planets...?
Mars
Mars' orbit
Sun

Kepler went on to develop a model which is the basis of our understanding of the solar system. Combined with Newton's laws of motion (see page 19), it enables astronomers to predict the movement of bodies in space with incredible accuracy.

The solar system

All objects in space that orbit the Sun are part of the solar system. Physicists have gathered all sorts of information about it from telescopes, probes and even robot rovers that beam back photos and detailed data via radio signals. Here is just some of that information.

Every object, from planets to satellites, is bound to the Sun by gravity. They travel around it in elliptical (oval) paths, at different distances and rates, but usually in a completely regular pattern.

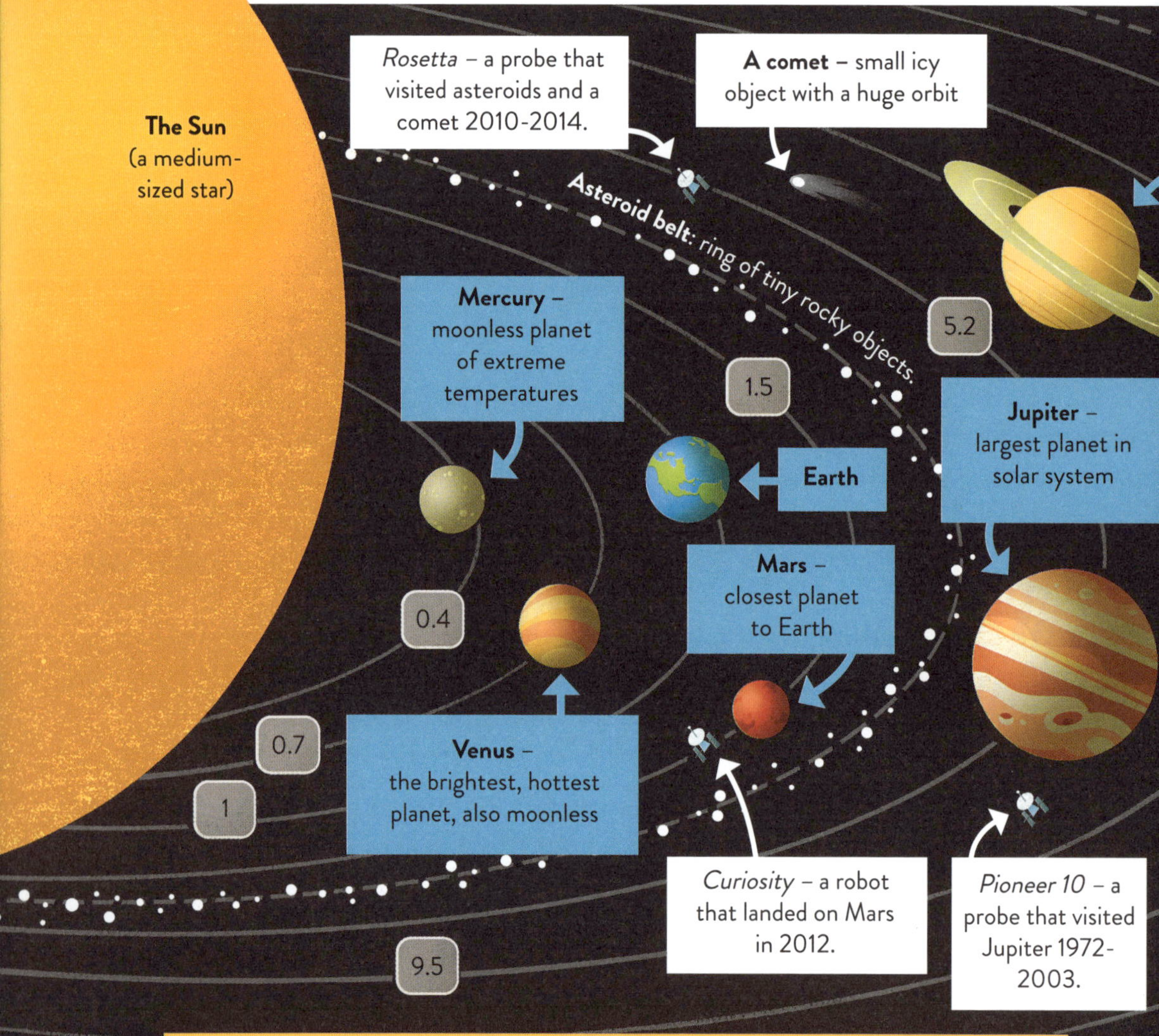

Key

Space probe or robot rover

Approximate average distance from the sun in **Astronomical Units**. 1 AU = 93 million miles

Dwarf planets

There are millions of asteroids in orbit around our Sun. These rocky objects can be as small as a pebble, or almost as big as our Moon. Some are irregular in shape; others are perfectly round. The largest round ones are known as dwarf planets and most are found in an area of space known as the **KUIPER BELT,** beyond Neptune.

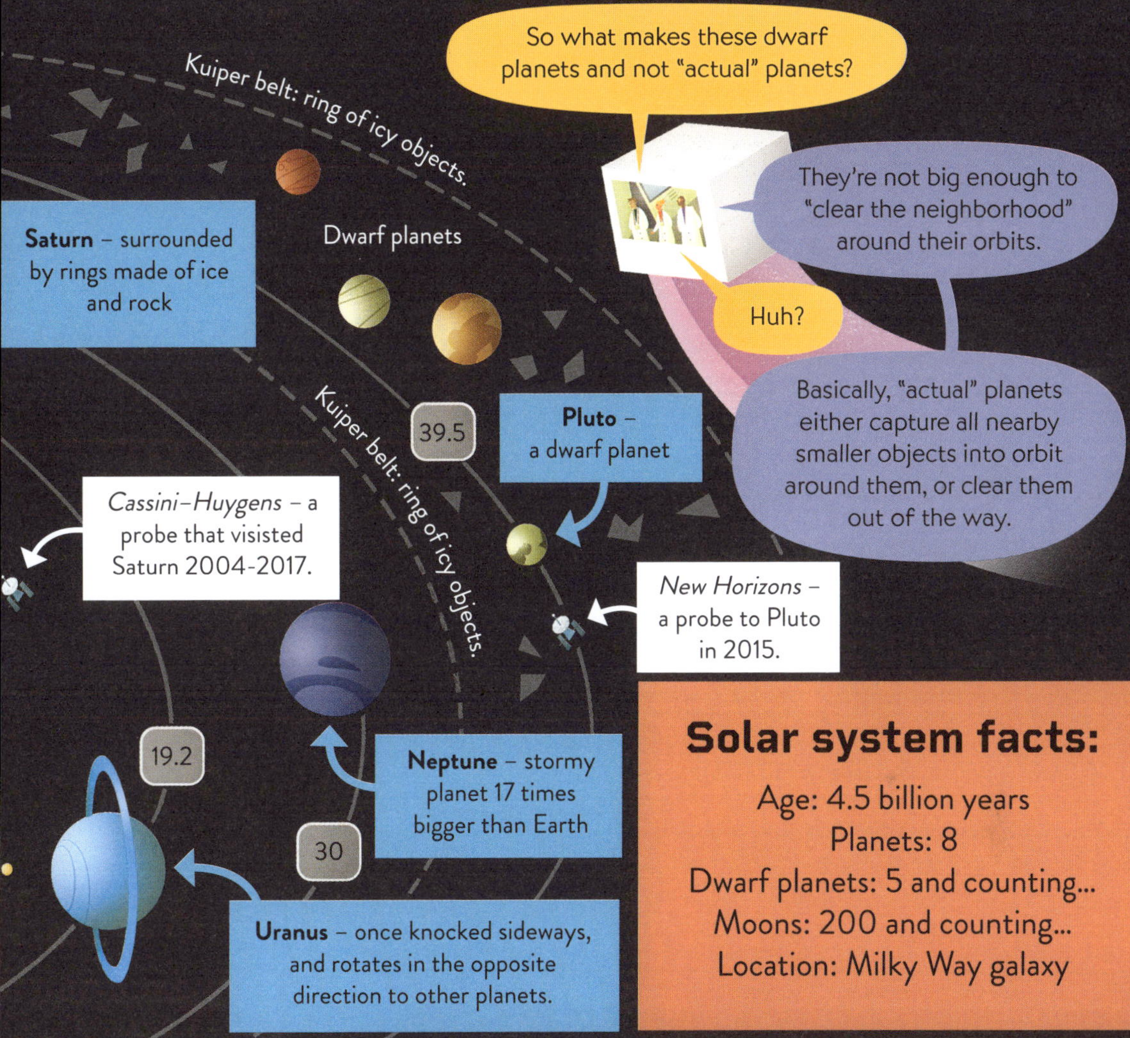

So what makes these dwarf planets and not "actual" planets?
They're not big enough to "clear the neighborhood" around their orbits.
Huh?
Basically, "actual" planets either capture all nearby smaller objects into orbit around them, or clear them out of the way.
Kuiper belt: ring of icy objects.
Dwarf planets
Saturn – surrounded by rings made of ice and rock
Kuiper belt: ring of icy objects.
39.5
Pluto – a dwarf planet
Cassini–Huygens – a probe that visited Saturn 2004-2017.
New Horizons – a probe to Pluto in 2015.
19.2
Neptune – stormy planet 17 times bigger than Earth
30
Uranus – once knocked sideways, and rotates in the opposite direction to other planets.

Solar system facts:

Age: 4.5 billion years
Planets: 8
Dwarf planets: 5 and counting...
Moons: 200 and counting...
Location: Milky Way galaxy

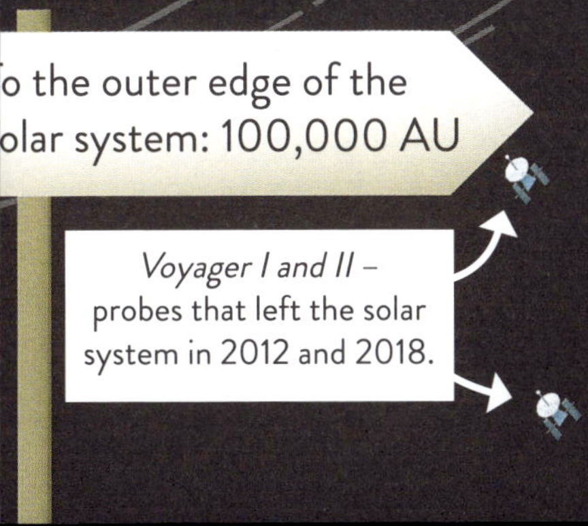

o the outer edge of the olar system: 100,000 AU
Voyager I and II – probes that left the solar system in 2012 and 2018.

Beyond the solar system

Our Sun is just one star amongst billions that exist in the universe. Most are very, very far away. But scientists have ways of studying stars without having to get anywhere near them. Turn the page to find out more.

Stars

There are hundreds of *billions* of stars in the universe. Most are so far away that they appear to us to be tiny lights in the sky, and we have little hope of ever getting close to them. And yet physicists know an astonishing amount about them. Here are some of the things they know.

Stars are massive balls of gas that produce vast amounts of heat and light.

They are all moving through space.

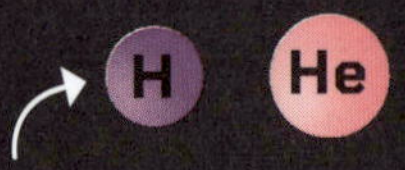

They are mainly made up of the gases hydrogen (H) and helium (He).

They have a life cycle that starts in a cloud of dust-like matter and can end with a massive explosion... or a slow fading away.

Learning from light

Our only contact with most stars is the light they send out. But this is enough to tell us all sorts of things. For a start, it can reveal what substances a star is made of. This is because all stars have a **LIGHT SIGNATURE**.

This is something physicists can observe because starlight, like all light, is made up of different wavelengths. They use instruments called **SPECTROMETERS** to capture those wavelengths. These show up as dark lines on a series of colorful strips. The dark lines, called absorption lines, are the star's light signature.

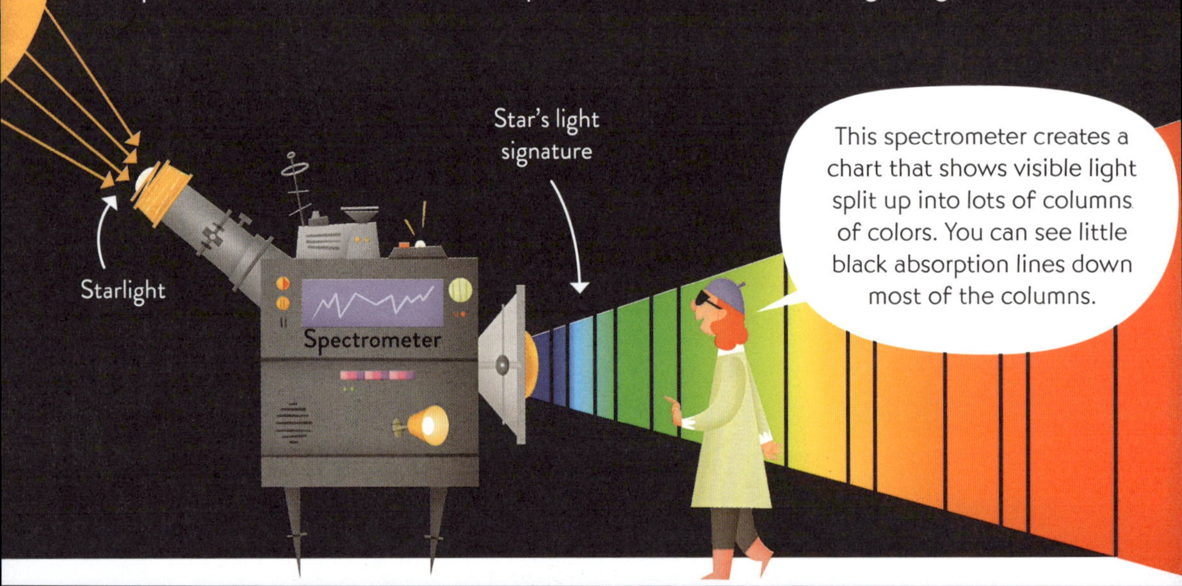

So how does this tell us what a star is made of? Well, certain substances give out unique patterns of wavelengths of light when they're hot. So, if you know which substances cause which patterns, you can work out which ones are present in a star by looking for these patterns in the star's signature.

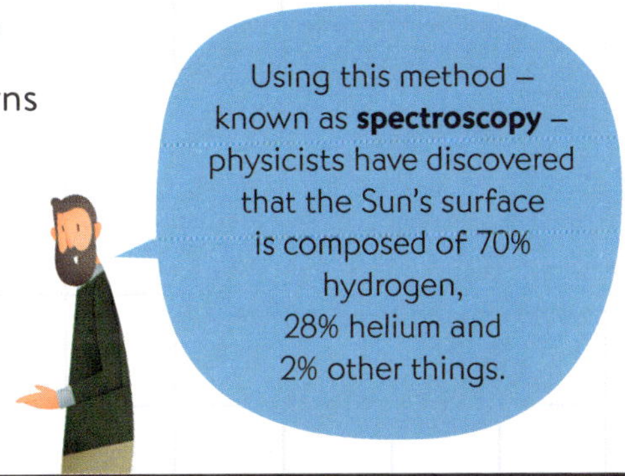
Using this method – known as **spectroscopy** – physicists have discovered that the Sun's surface is composed of 70% hydrogen, 28% helium and 2% other things.

Learning more from light

Physicists can find out many other things about stars by studying starlight, applying the laws of physics...

...and doing a lot of mathematics.

How far away is it?
How fast is it moving...
...and in what direction?
How big is it?
How bright is it?
How heavy is it?
How hot is it?

Star groups

In 1924, astronomer Annie Jump Cannon catalogued over 250,000 stars, based on their signatures and temperatures. She classified them all into seven main types – O, B, A, F, G, K, M – which are still used today.

G
Color: yellow
Temperature: about 8,500-10,340°F
Example: the Sun

M
Color: red
Temperature: under 5,840°F
Example: Betelgeuse

B
Color: medium blue
Temperature: 17,540-50,000°F
Example: Rigel

Black holes

Black holes are places in space, where space and time are warped to an infinite degree. Inside a black hole, gravity is so strong that nothing can escape it. And there is a supermassive one at the center of our own galaxy.

No escape

To take off from a planet, or indeed *any* massive body in space, there's a minimum speed you need to reach. This is called **escape velocity**. The larger the mass of an object, the higher its escape velocity. And black holes have such large masses that their escape velocity is faster than the speed of light. As it's impossible for anything to travel faster than light, *nothing* can escape a black hole.

Nothing?
Nothing. Not even light. That's why you can't see black holes directly. They suck in light rather than reflecting it.
So if we can't see black holes directly, how do we know they exist?
Well, black holes have pretty interesting effects on the things around them that we *can* see.
Before light is sucked into a black hole, it's bent around it.
This image shows light being bent around a black hole at the center of a galaxy called *Messier 87*.
That's the closest light can get to the black hole without hitting the **event horizon**. That's the point at which it's no longer possible to reach escape velocity.
The matter that makes up the black hole is in a tiny dot called a **singularity** in the middle of the black circle.

So... if there's a supermassive black hole at the center of our galaxy, why aren't we being sucked into it? We're not, are we...?
No. You'd have to be much, MUCH closer to it than we are before its gravity could pull you in. And you'd have to be right on top of it before you were actually sucked in.
Ok, so I have to ask. What *would* happen if you *were* sucked into a black hole?
Well physicists aren't certain, but it's not likely to end well.
As you approach the event horizon, time will speed up for you. But for people observing from a distance, you'd appear to slow down.
This is because of **relativity** (see page 43).
Then, a fraction of a second after crossing the event horizon, you'd undergo... ...spaghettification.
Spaghettification?! Is that a technical term?! Does it mean what I *think* it means?
Yes to both! Gravity will pull your feet away from your head and you'll be stretched out like a super-long, super-thin noodle.
Either that, or you'll just be killed instantly...
...but don't worry. You'd have to get really close, and the nearest black hole to Earth is 3,500 light years away.

Black hole physics

According to all established scientific theories, the normal laws of physics seem to break down inside black holes. So exactly *what* is happening in them and *why* remains a mystery. Many physicists believe that if they can solve this mystery, it may help to reveal the truth about the universe, and how it works.

The end of the universe

All good things come to an end, and the universe is no exception. But while most physicists agree that our universe and everything in it will eventually die, they don't all agree on *how* this will happen...

The End is coming! HEAT DEATH will be our... death.
The BIG RIP is upon us!
Forget that, what about the BIG CRUNCH!

Heat Death

The universe began with a sudden violent expansion, and since then it has never stopped expanding. If it keeps on doing this, everything in it will drift further and further apart. Stars will burn out and no new stars will form. Particles will eventually decay. In the end, all matter and energy will be evenly distributed. Nothing can change because nothing can interact. The universe will become a dark, cold, lifeless, still graveyard. This is known as **HEAT DEATH**.

So why's it called *Heat* Death, then? I was expecting a fiery inferno...
It means death *of* heat rather than death *by* heat. It's also sometimes known as the **Big Chill**.

But this is not the only possible way the universe might end. Here are some other theories.

The Big Rip

It's not just planets and stars that move away from one another as the universe expands. In the end, atoms, and even sub-atomic particles, will begin to tear apart too – and maybe even the very fabric of spacetime. If this happens, everything will be ripped apart and destroyed.

The Big Crunch

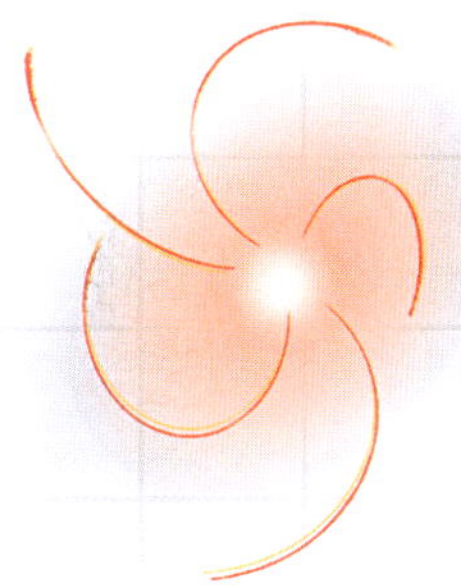

At some point, the universe will go into reverse. Gravity will overcome the force that's making the universe expand, and the universe will snap back like an elastic band. Everything will end up crunching together into a tiny, hot, dense point. (Sound familiar? Read on...)

BANG!
(again)

The Big Bounce

If the Big Crunch happens, the remaining tiny dense point will suddenly expand violently, resulting in the creation of the building blocks of matter... In other words, there will be *another Big Bang*. This could have already happened many, perhaps an infinite, number of times – there may not be a way of knowing if it has – and it may keep on happening forever.

Physicists currently think that Heat Death and the Big Rip are the most likely scenarios. But whatever the truth of the matter, the universe is not likely to end for many billions, or even trillions, of years.

Whew!

What's left to discover in space?

Is time travel possible?

What's a wormhole?

Can physics explain EVERYTHING?

Chapter 7
UNSOLVED MYSTERIES

Much of physics (not to mention science in general) is about wondering *how* and *why* things happen. However much we understand about our world, and the universe we live in, there are many details we simply do not understand, AT ALL.

Whether in a lab running experiments, or at a computer analyzing data, or simply observing the world around them, physicists are hoping to get closer to the truth. They want to know what everything's made of, why things happen the way they do, and how it all fits together.

If this sounds interesting to you, perhaps YOU could become a physicist, too.

Space travel

The farthest any human has traveled into space is to the Moon. Astronauts *could* make the seven-month trip to Mars using current technology (and an *awful* lot of money). But could they go any *further*?

With the fastest rocket built so far, it'd take *thousands* of years to reach our nearest star after the Sun, *Proxima Centauri.*

But the amount of fuel this would require doesn't exist, even if we wanted to do it.

So if we're going to travel to the stars, we'll need some radical new technology for our spacecraft.

I've heard physicists are working on at least four big ideas. Here they are.

Nuclear fusion engine

– powered by an onboard nuclear reactor

Pros: can reach 10% speed of light, cutting the journey time to 42 years to reach *Proxima Centauri.*
Cons: using current technology, nuclear fusion requires more energy than it produces.

Beam-powered propulsion

– powered by lasers, particle accelerators or even solar energy directed onto an on-ship light sail.

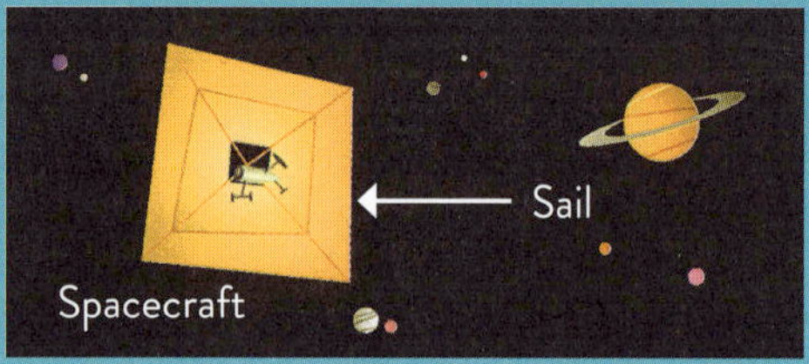

Pros: no need to carry any fuel.
Cons: to get enough speed, the sail needs to be rather BIG. No has yet worked out how to get such a gigantic object into space.

Antimatter drive

– powered by collisions between particles of matter and antimatter (Find out more on page 112.)

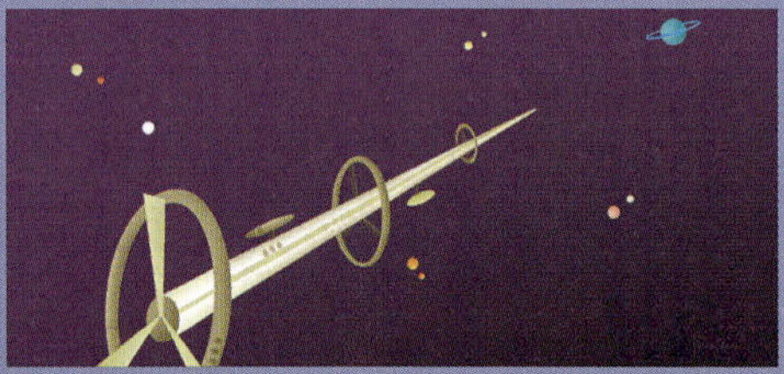

Pros: up to 90% speed of light: 4.6 years to reach *Proxima Centauri.*
Cons: physicists don't yet know how to produce and store antimatter in anything like the amounts needed, or in a safe way.

Alcubierre warp drive

– instead of powering the craft itself, the drive warps the space around the ship, cutting the total distance needed to travel.

Pros: could cut journey times down to a matter of hours.
Cons: no one has any idea how to do this. The concept is named after physicist Miguel Alcubierre, who has shown that it is, in theory, *possible.*

So traveling beyond our solar system doesn't look very promising.
Well, it depends on how quickly you want to get there. Have you heard of an idea called "suspended animation?"
It's when you put people into a deep sleep, keeping their bodies alive, without aging, for centuries. If we knew how to do that, people could fly through space on super-long journeys.
That's a big "if." And anyway, when they woke up, everyone and everything they knew would be likely to be gone!
That *is* a downside. But, there's one more trick physicists might try...

Taking a short cut

If spacecraft could move faster than light speed, a lot of the difficulties with interstellar travel would be resolved. But that's just not possible... is it? Well, yes and no. Theoretical physics predicts the possible existence of **wormholes** – shortcuts through spacetime that link two separate, distant points.

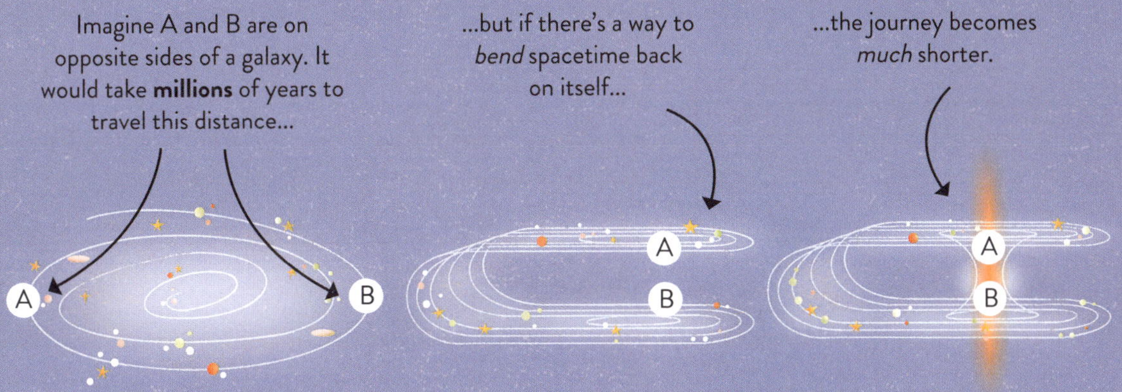
Imagine A and B are on opposite sides of a galaxy. It would take **millions** of years to travel this distance...
...but if there's a way to *bend* spacetime back on itself...
...the journey becomes *much* shorter.
A
B
A
B
A
B

Although you'd not actually be *moving* faster than light, you'd still get to your destination faster than light would, if it took the "normal" route around. But, you wouldn't just be moving through *space*, you'd also be moving through *time*...

Time travel

The universe isn't just space, it's space*time*. This means that opposite ends of a wormhole exist at different points in space *and* time. So going down one would potentially mean traveling back or forwards in time, *as well as* moving in space.

Tell me more... I want to try that!
Well, unfortunately, although *in principle* this could work, there are a few *practical* problems...
Firstly, you have to be able to find a wormhole. No one has actually found one yet.
Secondly, you need to be able to stretch it so that it's big enough to travel down. That would require a huge amount of *negative* energy... which may or may not exist.
Thirdly, we don't know if you could really pass through a wormhole and survive.
And even if we could do all this, there are the *philosophical* problems. Read on to find out more.

Physics and philosophy

There's one other rather big problem with time travel. It seems to be logically impossible. This means that, whatever physics states, time travel just *can't be done*. You might think this belongs in a philosophy book, not a physics one – but sometimes you can't do physics without doing a little philosophy too.

Consider this:

Jen's alarm clock doesn't go off because the battery's dead. She wakes up late and misses her math test.
Never mind! I'll just hop in my time machine... and go back to yesterday and replace the battery.
Jen replaces the battery, with what she thinks is a new one. (In fact, it's an old, dead one.)

In this story, Jen goes back in time to try to stop something from happening – but in doing so, she actually brings about the situation she's trying to avoid. It seems that all along, the alarm clock only *failed* to go off because she tried to *make sure* it *would* go off. This is what's known as a **paradox**. What Jen does seems to make sense, but it results in something that really *doesn't* seem to make sense.

But if she hadn't gone back in time, the alarm clock would have gone off so she wouldn't have missed the test in the first place.
Exactly!
I don't get it. It makes no sense.
No it doesn't, and that's the problem. But you can't rule out this sort of thing in principle when it comes to time travel...
...which suggests that the whole business of time travel is illogical and therefore... impossible.

Time travel sounds great, but it has a lot stacked against it. But at least the laws of physics *don't rule it out*. So will people ever do it? Only time will tell...

Matter and antimatter

While exploring the mathematics of subatomic particles, physicists found that their equations predicted something mysterious – the existence of particles of something they called **antimatter**.

The equations stated that ALL the particles of the Standard Model have an **antiparticle** partner.

Since 1955, physicists have managed to produce tiny amounts of antimatter in labs. But it never lasts very long.

I'm an electron –
I'm matter.
I'm an antielectron –
I'm antimatter.

Antimatter particles have the same mass as their matter particle twin, but are opposite to them in various ways. For instance, they have *opposite* electrical charges.

I have a negative charge.
+
-
I have a positive charge. You can call me **positron** if you like.

Danger: annihilation

Antimatter seems to be very rare. It takes huge amounts of energy to produce just a small amount – and storing it is even harder. That's because, when antimatter comes into contact with normal matter, both are **annihilated**.

When a positron meets an electron, they **destroy** each other.

Their mass is converted into energy...

...in the form of two photons.

Other annihilations produce different particles. All annihilations produce a huge amount of energy. Just 0.01oz of matter meeting 0.01oz of antimatter would produce the same energy as a small nuclear bomb. If we could do this safely, it could be a way to generate vast quantities of energy.

Where is all the antimatter?

One of the biggest mysteries in physics is why there's *so much* matter and *so little* antimatter out there.

As far as we understand it, the Big Bang should've created equal amounts of matter and antimatter...
...and they should have annihilated and left a universe filled with nothing but energy.
Yet the universe is FULL of matter, making up everything from cows to galaxies – but we can't see much antimatter at all. So what happened?
There might be more antimatter than you think. It's being created (and immediately destroyed) all the time in outer space, and even high up in Earth's atmosphere.
I heard on a podcast that there are *entire galaxies* made of antimatter. If that's true, we haven't seen them yet.
Well, we've discovered one thing that sets antimatter apart from matter: it seems to be affected differently by the *weak nuclear force* (see page 62).
I suppose that's a small clue. If you learn more about the weak force, do you think it'll solve the mystery of what happened to all the antimatter at the dawn of the universe?
Maybe? But it's also quite likely that some other thing was going on – during or just after the Big Bang – that had an effect as well. We've no idea what that was, though!
Oh. That must be frustrating.
Actually, I think it's rather exciting! Solving mysteries is why I became a physicist.

What the universe is made of

All the stuff in the universe that we can directly detect is made up of protons, neutrons and electrons, bundled together into atoms. But this makes up only 5% of the mass in the universe. So what's all the rest? Well, it's mysterious and it's invisible.

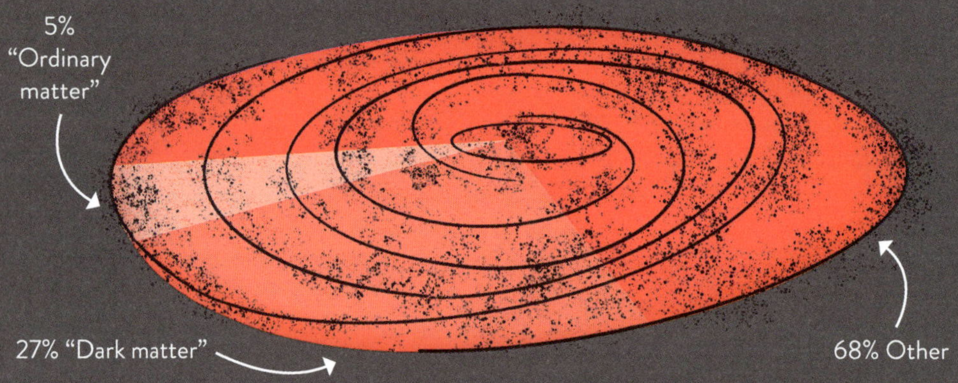

5% "Ordinary matter"
27% "Dark matter"
68% Other

No ordinary matter

Physicists think that about 27% of the universe is something they call **DARK MATTER**. Dark matter doesn't interact with "ordinary" matter directly. Nor does it interact with anything on the electromagnetic spectrum (see page 38). So it's impossible to detect directly using any instruments we have yet invented.

So what is it exactly?
We don't know. We know what it's *not* – it's not gas or black holes. But beyond that... it could be some new, undiscovered fundamental particle? But whatever it is, physicists think that it's all over the universe.
Okaaay. So what makes physicists think it exists, given that we can't detect it directly?
Because dark matter could explain lots of different things that just don't fit in with the laws of physics as we understand them. These are mainly to do with gravity. Read on for an example...

The great galactic gravity conundrum

Most stars exist in vast groups known as **galaxies**. What keeps stars – along with gases, dust, ice and other bits – in their galaxy is **gravity**. Very large objects tend to rotate around the center. Current theories suggest that the farther from the center they are, the more slowly they should rotate. But they don't.

What if...
...there were some *other source* of gravity in our galaxy?
Could be. One theory says there's a source of gravity not *within*, but *surrounding*, our galaxy, like a halo. This might explain the way stars rotate.
Ooh, that's an interesting idea. Let's say you're right, and let's imagine that halo is made of DARK MATTER.
OK! So in theory, this dark matter interacts with *ordinary* matter through gravity. We just need to find a way to observe that happening in more detail.
Our galaxy
Halo of dark matter
If there IS a galactic gravity halo, it would also explain a few other mysteries.
For example, why galaxies don't fly apart, and those curious gravitational lensing effects (see page 51).

What else is the universe is made of?

Frankly, we don't know. Based on current theories, the universe should have stopped expanding, but it hasn't – in fact, it's expanding faster than ever. In a vague attempt to explain this, physicists point to an unknown factor they call **dark energy**. Tantalizing clues about dark energy have recently been detected by people studying muons. But those clues may turn out to be errors in the equipment used to measure them. So we still don't really know.

Bringing it all together

One of the dreams of physics is a **unified theory** – a single explanation that can be used to describe *everything*. Physicists have come pretty far, but they've run into a problem...

We currently have two theories that describe the universe brilliantly.

But they don't seem to make sense together.

GENERAL RELATIVITY	Vs	QUANTUM MECHANICS
Describes gravity, planets, galaxies and the massive objects in the universe.		Describes incredibly tiny particles that make up matter, and the interactions between them.

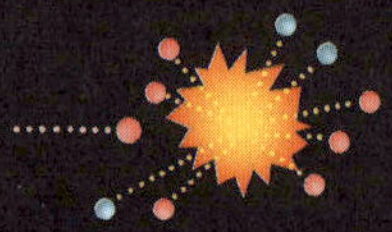

You say that quantum mechanics explains a lot of things. But quantum *effects* vanish when we talk about the everyday objects that gravity affects – from rocks to people to planets.

Well your equations from general relativity give answers that don't make sense when we apply them to things on the quantum scale.

But gravity affects ALL matter – and all matter is made of fundamental particles so... the two theories *must* work together somehow.

Either we're missing something – or one of the two theories is wrong, even though they both work really well!

What if...?

Many "theories of everything" predict that the fundamental particles from the Standard Model might be made of something *even smaller*. These smaller objects haven't been *proved* to exist, but some physicists have an idea of what they might be.

String theory

The idea: all the particles – at least, the particles described by the Standard Model – are actually miniscule "strings" of energy, vibrating at different frequencies.

It's like playing a guitar. Changing the length of the string changes the frequency it vibrates at, and the note it plays.
Pros: the math for string theory manages to make sense of both general relativity AND quantum mechanics.
Cons: the theory states that the universe is made of at least eleven dimensions. But we've only ever found evidence of four: length, width, depth and time.
Frankly, a lot of physicists think string theory SOUNDS neat, but aren't convinced by it.

For scientists to be able to observe strings directly, they'd need to design and power a particle accelerator far beyond anything we can build today. For many physicists, unified theories are little more than mathematical thought experiments. Proving any of them by doing experiments isn't possible... YET.

Would you like to know more?

There are more things that we DON'T know about the universe than we do know. Explore this web to find out which branches of physics might interest YOU most – and perhaps you will help solve a mystery in the future...

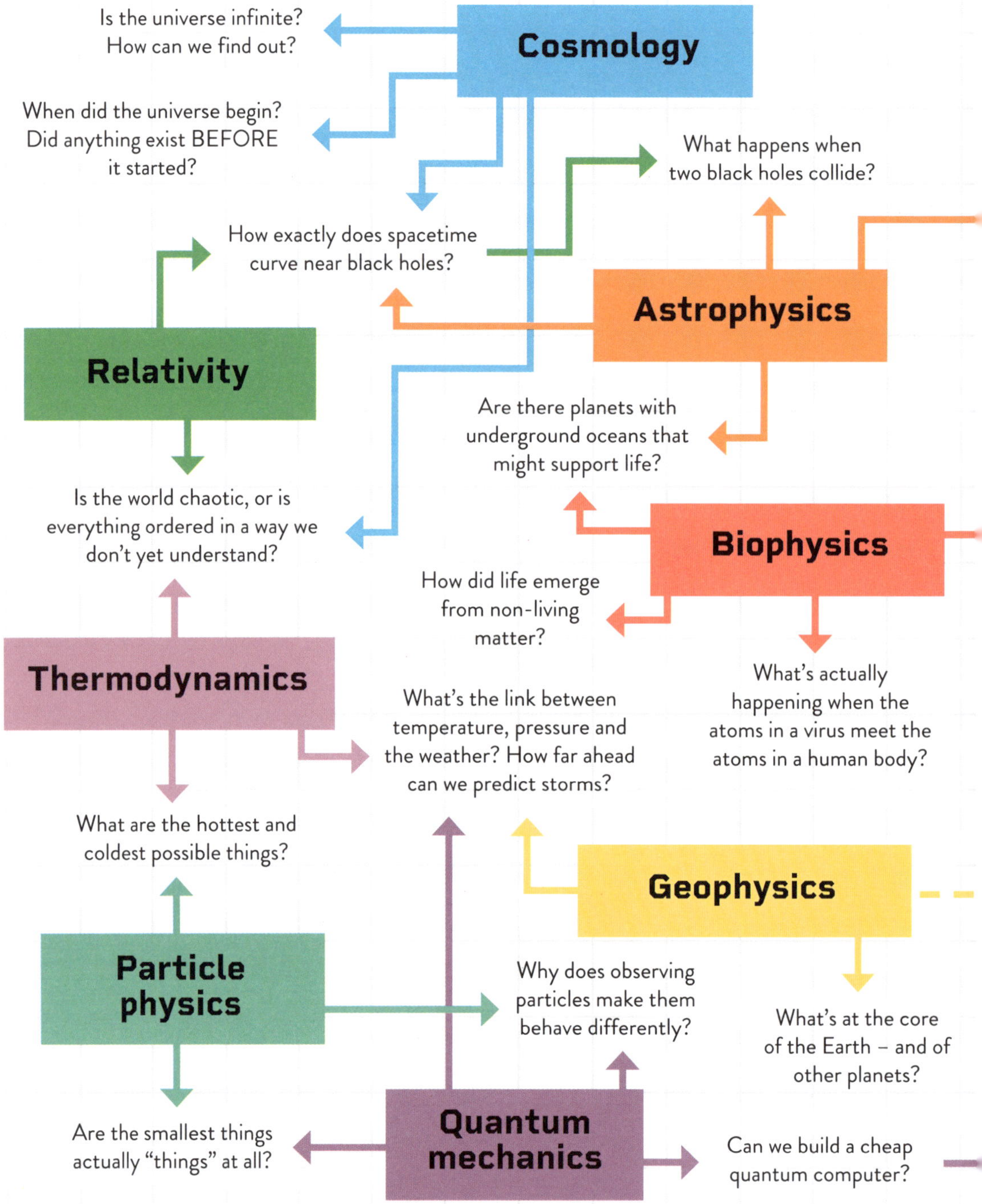

Cosmology
Is the universe infinite? How can we find out?
When did the universe begin? Did anything exist BEFORE it started?
How exactly does spacetime curve near black holes?
What happens when two black holes collide?
Astrophysics
Relativity
Are there planets with underground oceans that might support life?
Is the world chaotic, or is everything ordered in a way we don't yet understand?
Biophysics
How did life emerge from non-living matter?
Thermodynamics
What's actually happening when the atoms in a virus meet the atoms in a human body?
What's the link between temperature, pressure and the weather? How far ahead can we predict storms?
What are the hottest and coldest possible things?
Geophysics
Particle physics
Why does observing particles make them behave differently?
What's at the core of the Earth – and of other planets?
Are the smallest things actually "things" at all?
Quantum mechanics
Can we build a cheap quantum computer?

Can we build a better world?

As well as answering all kinds of questions about the world, physics also helps to solve specific problems. Engineers use discoveries and equations from all across physics to help develop and construct practical inventions.

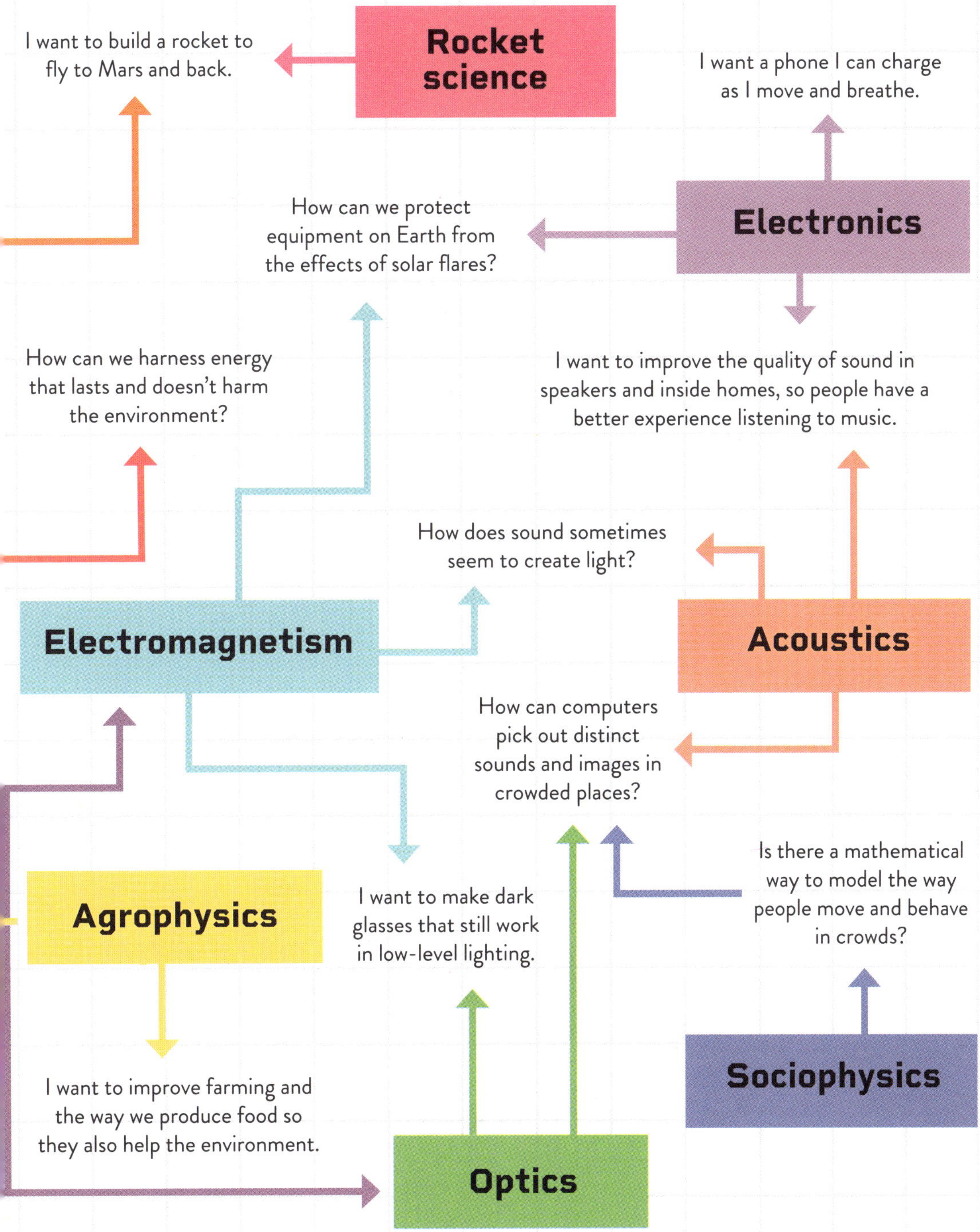

Rocket science
I want to build a rocket to fly to Mars and back.
Electronics
I want a phone I can charge as I move and breathe.
How can we protect equipment on Earth from the effects of solar flares?
I want to improve the quality of sound in speakers and inside homes, so people have a better experience listening to music.
How can we harness energy that lasts and doesn't harm the environment?
Electromagnetism
How does sound sometimes seem to create light?
Acoustics
How can computers pick out distinct sounds and images in crowded places?
Is there a mathematical way to model the way people move and behave in crowds?
Agrophysics
I want to make dark glasses that still work in low-level lighting.
Sociophysics
I want to improve farming and the way we produce food so they also help the environment.
Optics

How to do physics yourself

Physicists ask HOW and WHY things happen, and do experiments to test their ideas. You can do this, too, and you don't need fancy equipment. You might be reading, watering plants, watching a movie or visiting a museum when something sparks an idea...

Light
Ah, the rainbow only appears when sunlight hits the spray at a certain angle...
Look! I can make light bend in lots of ways. But what makes each color bend at different angles?

Forces
That eagle doesn't even have to flap its wings to fly...
What if I copy the wing shape on this piece of paper?
Fwoosh
Easier said than done, I guess.

Static electricity
After rubbing this ruler on my sweater, I can make the flow of water move without touching it.
Wow!
I can collect dust in the air using the static energy on this ruler.
Hmm, this could be a way to get rid of pollution on our streets.

Relativity

Hey, you're really stuck in the past. Since flying for 10 hours, my watch is 0.05 seconds faster than yours.
Wow! Time went faster for her...
So if she went into the future, maybe it's possible to go *back* in time, too...

Quantum mechanics

Ah! Which way should we go?
If only we could try out two paths at once.
Hey, subatomic particles can do this already – maybe we could build a miniscule *quantum robot* that can do it, too...

Over to you

Wherever you are, sitting at home, going for a walk, doing a job, relaxing with friends, look around. Almost everything you observe can be explained with physics. But there is also so much more left to be explained – which is what makes it such an AMAZING subject.

Glossary

This glossary explains some of the words used in this book.
Words in *italics* are explained in other entries.

atoms collections of particles which make up *matter*.

black hole a hole in the fabric of *spacetime*, left when large stars die.
Big Bang, the the event that caused the expansion of *the universe*.

charge a property that some kinds of particles can have, described as either "positive" or "negative."
Cosmic Microwave Background Radiation (CMBR) traces of extreme heat left over from the *Big Bang*.

dark matter unknown type of *matter* that makes up 27% of the *universe*.
density how tightly packed together the *atoms* are in an object.

$E=mc^2$ the *equation* that shows that *matter* and *energy* are the same thing.
electromagnetism the *force* that describes electricity and magnetism.
electromagnetic spectrum the range of electromagnetic waves caused by vibrating *photons*.
electrons negatively charged *fundamental particles* that cause electrical currents and orbit *atom*s.
energy the ability of *matter* to move or change.
entropy the tendency for things to go from ordered to chaos.

force a push or a pull that causes an object to move or change.
frequency the number of waves emitted by a source of *energy*, per second.
friction resistance caused by two things moving against each other.
fundamental particles the smallest building blocks of the universe, which interact to form *matter* and *energy*.

General Relativity a *theory* that describes *gravity* as a bending of *spacetime*.
gluons the *fundamental particles* that hold *atoms* together.
gravity the *force* that causes attraction between *matter*.

Higgs bosons *fundamental particles* that give all *matter* its *mass*.

inertia the tendency for an object to stay still or at a steady speed if no *force* is acting on it.

kinetic energy the energy of a moving object.

mass the amount of *matter* an object contains.
matter anything made up of *atoms*.
momentum the speed and direction an object is moving in.

muons *fundamental particles* similar to *electrons*, but with more *mass*.

neutrons the neutrally *charged* parts of an *atom*'s *nucleus*.
nucleus the core of an *atom* (plural: *nuclei*).
nuclear fission releasing *energy* by splitting the *nucleus* of an *atom* open.
nuclear fusion releasing *energy* by fusing the *nuclei* of *atoms* together.

particle accelerator a machine used to break open *matter* to study *fundamental particles*.
photons *fundamental particles* of light and the *electromagnetic spectrum*.
protons the positively *charged* parts of an *atom*'s *nucleus*.

quantum the smallest amount of *energy* possible (plural: *quanta*). All subatomic particles are quanta of different types of *energy*.
quantum mechanics the branch of physics that describes the behavior of *fundamental particles*.
quarks the *fundamental particles* that form *protons* and *neutrons*.

radioactivity a property of unstable *atom*s to decay into more stable atoms via the *weak nuclear force*.
redshift the change in *frequency* of light from a moving source, causing it to change color.

solar system, the the collection of planets and other objects that orbit the Sun.
spacetime the fabric of the *universe* that is made of the dimensions of space (height, depth and width) and time.
Special Relativity a *theory* linking space and time into *spacetime*, it states that the speed of light is the fastest speed possible.
Standard Model, the a *theory* describing all known *fundamental particles* and their interactions with each other.
strong nuclear force a *force* that holds the *nucleus* of an *atom* together.

theory an explanation for why things happen that is backed up by the evidence people have found so far.

universe, the everything we can see, feel and detect, from tiny *fundamental particles* to gigantic galaxies.

visible light part of the *electromagnetic spectrum* that can be seen by the human eye.

W boson a *fundamental particle* that allows *radioactive atoms* to stabilize.
wavelength the distance between the highest points of two waves.
weak nuclear force a *force* that allows *radioactive atom*s to stabilize by emiting a *w boson*.

Index

Jobs from physics

As well as exploring the mysteries of the universe, people who study physics can find all sorts of jobs outside of labs and universities.

architects design all kinds of buildings.

clinical scientists work with doctors to develop and test medical technology

engineers help to design, plan and even build things, from bridges to rockets to computer programs.

environment artists design worlds and write computer code to create artificial places that obey the rules of physics.

forensic scientists work with detectives and attorneys to investigate what happened at crime scenes.

mechanics design and repair all kinds of machines.

meteorologists study and predict the weather.

neuroscientists study and model how brains work at the smallest level.

patent agents examine new inventions to determine if they are new and different to any previous inventions.

science journalists research and explain new discoveries in science in a way that can be understood by non-scientists.

systems analysts analyze, design and organize ways of working, which might involve groups of computers or teams of people.

Acknowledgements

Written by
Rachel Firth, Minna Lacey
and Darran Stobbart

Illustrated by
El Primo Ramón

Edited by
Alex Frith

Designed by
Jamie Ball

Series editor:
Jane Chisholm

Physics expert:
Daisy Shearer MPhys,
University of Surrey's
Advanced Technology Institute

Series designer:
Stephen Moncrieff

The websites recommended at Usborne Quicklinks are regularly reviewed but Usborne Publishing is not responsible and does not accept liability for the availability or content of any website other than its own, or for any exposure to harmful, offensive or inaccurate material which may appear on the Web. Usborne Publishing will have no liability for any damage or loss caused by viruses that may be downloaded as a result of browsing the sites it recommends.

First published in 2022 by Usborne Publishing Limited,
83-85 Saffron Hill, London EC1N 8RT, United Kingdom. usborne.com
Copyright © 2022 Usborne Publishing Limited. The name Usborne and the Balloon logo are registered trade marks of Usborne Publishing Limited. All rights reserved. No part of this publication may be reproduced or used in any manner for the purpose of training artificial intelligence technologies or systems (including for text or data mining), stored in retrieval systems or transmitted in any form or by any means without prior permission of the publisher.
First published in America 2022. This edition published 2025. AE.